ARE YOU A PEOPLE-PLEASER?

HOW TO BUILD ASSERTIVENESS, GAIN RESPECT AND STOP PEOPLE-PLEASING

FREDDIE MALLIN

CONTENTS

INTRODUCTION

If you always care about what other people think, you will always be their prisoner.

— LAO TZU

When you truly have a big heart and care about other people, you will have people-pleasing tendencies you need to heal. It is part of the challenge of having a big heart. The key to dealing with this toxic habit, though, is not to close your heart down or to stop caring, but to focus your care where it belongs—on yourself. Let me back-track.

Being someone who pleases other people sounds, on the face of it, like a good idea. Yet, it is a behavior pattern riddled with problems for both the perpetrator and the audience. A people-pleaser is someone who feels that they have no choice but to shape themselves to meet other people's expectations and yet harbors many secret and dangerous resentments and reservations. They want everyone around them to be happy and do whatever it takes to keep it that way. The people-pleaser acts like the perfect lover when their feelings are darker; they agree to plans they hate; they confuse all those around them by failing to voice their authentic needs and ambitions in good time and with the needed courage. One could say that a people-pleaser is a practiced liar. It sounds brutal, but people-pleasing is lying for reasons other than the usual ones. The people-pleaser is not out to gain an advantage but is so afraid of displeasing others that they shy away from the truth—at least their version of it. They can be perfectionists who rehearse everything they will say before a phone call, who spend hours on the internet researching the perfect shoe that "defines" them, or who style their hair meticulously in the mirror. For some, saying yes is a habit. For others, it is an addiction. They feel useful and needed when they are validated for being a people-pleaser.

To understand where the people-pleaser is coming from, you have to look into their past. Almost invariably, the people-pleaser was around people, often parents, who appeared radically incapable of accepting and forgiving certain traits about the child. It could be that your father flew into a volcanic rage whenever there was a small disagreement. To present an opposing idea, suggest you wanted to eat something different, or be honest about your tiredness could threaten you with annihilation. To survive, you had to become responsive to what was expected of you. The question of what you might want always came second to others—second-guessing the needs of those whom your life depended upon.

You did not lie because you were afraid; it was often out of love for someone you were attached to who was vulnerable somehow. You lied to prevent your parents from fighting, to keep a parent in a good mood, or to avoid adding another burden to what already seemed like a sad life. Why would you want to make things more difficult for someone for whom you cared?

However understandable your behavior's origins are, though, you have long left that stage in life where you needed to lie to survive. You are an adult now. Yet you find that people-pleasing has become reflexive in your adulthood. You say yes to everything and everyone. You are always seeking validation, always wondering if people like you, and no matter what you try, you have been unable to shake this habit.

There are three paths away from people-pleasing. The first one lies in knowing that our colleagues, friends, and family members are different from the people that we grew up around. Most people can cope well with a little contradiction, an occasional rejection, and a dose of unwelcome information if delivered well. Knowing that your friends will not dissolve or explode can be the first step to put you at ease. It could start you down the path of recognizing that you learned a peculiar habit from people who did not represent the whole of humanity.

The second path out of people-pleasing lies in the acknowledgment of the harmful effects of this behavior. You may sincerely have good intentions but you are putting everyone around you in danger by not speaking openly. At work, you are not doing anyone a favor by withholding your reservations or doubts. In love, there is no kindness in staying in a relationship out of the fear that the other person might not survive without you. Your sentimentality ends up wasting a lot of time.

Thirdly, you can get out of people-pleasing by mastering the confidence to be artful about the difficult conversations you need to have. As a child, you did not have the skillset to nuance the messages you wanted to send. You did not know how to craft your raw pain and how to package your needs into convincing explanations. Now, as an adult, it is up to you to be firm with your views, but genial. You can learn to say no while indicating that you have a lot of goodwill; you can communicate that someone is wrong about something without suggesting that they are an idiot. You can leave someone while making sure they realize how much the relationship meant to you. In other words, you can be pleasant without being a people-pleaser.

Years ago, I was a recovering awkward person. I was completely burned out on people. I did not have great friends with whom I could have amazing conversations. I constantly felt overextended. It took courage to find my voice and to use it. I had to master how to set boundaries and to stop being a people-pleaser. I had to take control of my life and surrender to the truth that the only person I had to please was me. After working on myself, I no longer have to pretend to agree with everyone. I know I am not responsible for how other people feel. I can say no, and I can speak confidently about the things I want. The skills I learned have helped me to build a successful career in investment banking. In my line of work, gaining respect and being assertive is a requirement. Through years of study and plenty of research, I have come to understand people-pleasing and recover from it through the tools I will discuss in this book. I want to help you to overcome the mental barriers that stand in the way of your social and career development.

Here, you will learn how to put meeting your own needs and happiness before others. You will learn to fill your cup first and out of its overflow, to pour into other people's cups. Your well-being will become the priority of your focus. You will be able to operate with your energy on full and to show up to care for others from your heart. Feeling drained, exhausted, violated, resentful, and unhappy with life will be a thing of the past. I will show you that it is a blessing to have a big heart: the curse is not taking care of it well.

If this sounds like what you want—to care for others from a place of self-love and not self-sacrifice—read on.

1

NEEDING TO PLEASE

People-pleasers are excellent at pleasing everyone, but themselves. They are master accommodators. They intuitively know what is expected of them in deed and word and give their attention and care to others while typically denying themselves the same. They defer to the preferences of others so frequently that they lose sight of their own. According to them, their value in life is based on how valuable they are to others. As such, people-pleasers are adept at nurturing those around them, but they have no idea how to nurture themselves. Since safeguarding relationships is how they have learned to prop up their fragile egos, they cannot recognize the ultimate cost of devoting themselves to others' welfare. They do not acknowledge that there is nothing noble in sacrificing their selfhood.

The people-pleaser imagines that their security hinges on pleasing and appeasing others. They do this so much that it becomes a habit, and they soon forget what they need to feel fulfilled. They are so dependent on others' acceptance and approval that they are incapable of validating themselves without others' confirmation. The people-pleaser fears to speak their mind if their preferences and opinions are at odds with whomever they are with, which means that they are indecisive and afraid to take the initiative or make any difference.

In their unceasing efforts to avoid confrontation and conflict and to get along with everyone, people-pleasers rarely express their true feelings and thoughts. They frequently do not even know what they believe and what is important to them. They are chameleons who endeavor to blend in as much as they can with the people they are with. Being subordinate to those they are around, they attract people with a strong need to dominate, consequently magnifying a too-servile demeanor to start with. People-pleasers typically have unresolved issues with their parents, which cause them to be attracted to manipulative and domineering people, creating a situation that perpetuates old patterns. Before delving into the psychology of the people-pleaser, it helps to define terminologies.

Most websites you will find online summarize people-pleasers by enumerating their characteristics, and while that is helpful, it pays to know what the experts have said about the term. Is people-pleasing a character trait or a personality? Are there people who are more inclined to people-please than others?

How does people-pleasing co-exist with other traits? What causes people-pleasing tendencies?

In psychology, people-pleasing behavior is typically referred to as sociotropy. Such a person tends to consider relationships with others to be more important than their independence. The impression or appearance that the people-pleaser makes, though, is primarily a façade. They try hard to make other people happy, but they do this because of their lack of self-esteem and insecurities. Since their behavior is rooted in issues of self-worth, the people-pleaser hopes that if they agree to everything required of them, they will be liked and accepted.

Many people-pleasers confuse pleasing people with kindness. They imagine that in saying "no," they are selfish. Others commonly give responses like, "I want to be a good person." The result is that other people take advantage of them. Sociotropy can be seen as the opposite of autonomy because people with sociotropy care more about interpersonal relationships. Autonomy is more concerned with independence and does not care so much about other people. No wonder sociotropy has been correlated with some personalities and with feminine sex-role orientation in many studies.

In his 1983 paper Cognitive Therapy of Depression, Beck, A.T. hypothesized that sociotropy and autonomy concerns are connected to vulnerabilities and depression when a person experiences traumatic events. These personality constructs relate differently to different symptoms of depression. Recent research suggests that sociotropy is related to anxiety symptoms and depression, while autonomy is related to the symptoms of depression. The research further found that sociotropy moderated how achievement and interpersonal stress relate to symptoms of depression.

The research begs the question of whether there is a people-pleaser personality. Research has found that people higher in agreeableness tend to be more prone to people-pleasing than other personality types. Women are often higher in agreeableness than men, which means that there is a considerable tendency for women to be people-pleasers. Beck's research sought to explore how far the overlap between sociotropy, autonomy, and sexual orientation goes. Researchers examined six measures of sex-role orientation using a sample of 153 people. Ninety-five of the group were women, and 58 were men with a mean age of 20 years. True to suspicions, sociotropy was connected with the feminine factor, and autonomy was connected firmly to the masculine factor.

The mean score was higher for women than for men on sociotropy, but the difference in autonomy was not significant. The findings suggest that there is a definitional overlap between sex-role orientation and vulnerability to depression. In his 1991 paper Generation of Stress in the Course of Unipolar Depression, Constance Hammen proposed that both autonomy and sociotropy may explain the process of stress generation and the contribution each individual makes to a stressful environment.

Even so, more research is needed to differentiate different vulnerability factors. The research was conclusive, though, regarding gender and sociotropy—being female and scoring high on sociotropy predicted higher stress levels from interpersonal relationships. Still, people-pleasing behavior is not just found in women. Men, too, have been found to exhibit sociotropy.

People-pleasing sounds innocuous enough, bringing to mind the image of a happy, well-meaning person, or perhaps an ordinary person who is just a little needy. You may wonder what the problem might be with being a people-pleaser. What is wrong with wanting other people to be happy, you may ask? Does it affect the people-pleasers in any way? Gary Vaynerchuk wrote a book on sociotropy in which he argued that being a people-pleaser is a strength, not a weakness. The truth, though, is that people-pleasing is much darker and far more profound than you may imagine.

Do not get me wrong—people-pleasing can give you some advantages. It could even look like a superpower. As an employee, you may become a star: the person always picked to handle difficult situations, the warrior on the frontline who is always graceful under pressure, the person who gets things done. In relationships, people-pleasing can make you the effortless, perfect partner, regardless of whether you are dating a demanding person, an academic, a hedge fund manager, or an athlete. You are cool with all of them, entirely in sync, undemanding, and genuine—never a push-over, just a version of yourself tailor-made for them.

Think of this example: Peter is a classic people-pleaser. He has been dating Lesley for four years and is hoping that they will marry. From the start, Lesley wanted Peter to go to church with her and finish college. Peter is not interested in church and is unsure whether he believes in God but attends church anyway. He left college when he was a freshman and is sure that he is not interested in returning. Rather than letting Lesley know, he makes excuses for not enrolling. He works for his father's company and is in discussions with his father about taking over the business. Peter feels stuck. He fears telling his girlfriend and his dad what he wants. Most of the time, he does not even know what he wants, and so, despite being unhappy, he goes along instead of risking his father's disappointment or a breakup with Lesley. Peter is the perfect example of a people-pleaser. He fears rejection and abandonment. Hiding his needs has become a survival skill for him.

People-pleasing is often tied to perfectionism. It is about appearing perfect to the onlooker. If you figure out the needs of others and meet them, they will be pleased with you. They might even love you, and that will prove your worth. Yet, people-pleasing is inevitably tied to the following problems:

It is impossible to please everyone.

A people-pleaser creates an impossible situation. Trying to please everyone means that they are always complaining. They never disagree, and yet it is impossible to please some people even if you do exactly as they ask. What is more, people-pleasing can go unnoticed, even by the sociotrope. Such self-delusion is more common with women because the trait is gender normative. You end up in environments where no one is honest enough to point out when things are not okay. The people-pleaser develops an overly sunny personality to mask their lack of decisiveness. Others take on a sarcastic tone and flippant attitude that may protect them from being detected.

Internally, the people-pleaser is constantly at odds with the façade they choose to wear. For one, they will not value their constant friendliness. They unconsciously feel it to be a choice to surrender their freedom—heaven forbid they disappoint someone. In a moment of half-clarity, the people-pleaser may see someone they admire speaking their mind and try to mimic their attitude. They express themselves a few times, and when things do not go as they hoped, they decide that it is not worth the effort. Often, things fail to go their way because they hardly take the time to figure out what they want, meaning that their uncertainty is always detectable beneath their half-hearted attempt at self-assertion.

In efforts to deal with the frustration they feel at not being able to please everyone, other people-pleasers find socially acceptable outlets. They may volunteer for what appears to be noble causes like working with refugees. Such fields tend to be filled with obvious do-gooders. The people-pleaser, at this point, convinces themselves that such is the nature of life, and they go on, always making nice with people and yet never genuinely meaning it until they experience burnout that, if they are fortunate, teaches them the lesson that it is impossible to please everyone.

1. In people-pleasing, you lose yourself.

Like Peter, when you focus on people-pleasing, you lose sight of the things you value, your personality, and your goals. This means that you can never stand up for your beliefs or go after your dreams. Your true self becomes buried beneath the people-pleaser. In the beginning, people-pleasing seems like a worthy trade-off. On the surface, you think that it will not hurt you. After all, things run smoothly. You have no fights, no fussing, and no conflict. In relationships, no one will dump you—no one will fault you. You start to think that reality is a sign of your character strength, yet you are gaming the system.

Under the surface, you start to experience the effects of your pretense. You begin to experience less emotionally because you do not want to own yourself and see things through your eyes. It starts to become second nature to scope things out through everyone around you, measuring how happy you are through others. You become unable to love. What is love when you are using emotional control tools on your partner all the time, even if they do not know it? What is love if you constantly indulge those you claim to love without being sure that you want to?

Having lost themselves, many people-pleasers become manipulative. They learn to turn situations their way using words and under the guise of kindness or defense of the underdog. They are, in their eyes, always trying to make things fairer. It never occurs to them that they are anything other than good. Thinking of themselves as good people is more flattering than acknowledging their compulsion to please and the loss of identity that comes as a result.

Another group of people-pleasers gives their life to things that they have no interest in. A woman could spend her twenties jumping from tour to tour, moving to random places where she is not known, always leaving but never arriving at a place where she is satisfied. People-pleasers instinctively are, do, and say things that, even if accurate, are meant to comfort others. They forget how to be around people without getting disfigured by their people-pleasing tendencies. After trying to put on a face for so long, they are worn out, and they remove the mask, except, they no longer remember who they are or what they want. The realization that the people-pleaser does not know himself sends them to another place, searching for an escape. He believes, without realizing it, that everywhere he goes, there he is, and yet is constantly dumbfounded at the emptiness he finds in himself if he dares to look.

2. You tie your worth to pleasing others.

As you continue people-pleasing, you come to believe that if you do not please other people, they will leave, reject, or belittle you. You have created a situation in which you feel unlovable and unworthy when others are not pleased with you. As a result, you meet every situation with the compulsive need to avoid conflict. True, most people would prefer being liked to conflict, but the people-pleaser goes beyond being good-natured. Whereas a healthy person can deal with varied approaches tailored for the situations they are in, the people-pleaser meets every situation with just one default—the compulsive need to impress.

You can think of the people-pleasers actions as an elaborate dance choreographed to avoid conflict. For them, provocative emotions like anger are special. While good-natured people can get angry, people-pleasers do not get angry. They could become sad, depressed, or suicidal, but never angry. They repress their full emotional range because the need to be validated trumps everything else.

The sociotrope does not just repress their anger—they go out of their way to assuage other people's unpleasant feelings. The more adept the people-pleaser is, the better they play the emotional detective's role, quick to ferret out other people's displeasure before they express it. They patch things up before the heat is turned up. They mitigate your worries about things you had not even thought about. They do this because they are afraid that someone will get upset at them, and deem them unworthy of affection. When the need to be validated becomes so strong, it gets conflated with self-worth, and codependence begins to take root.

Sociotropy is a socially acceptable way of hiding trauma in plain sight. It is the unwillingness to use one's full emotional range, and it points to old wounds that were too painful to deal with. In relying on others to determine your worth, you exhibit your trauma in a way that goes unnoticed. You constantly smooth things over with niceness to hide in plain sight. After all, who will complain when you are helping others? No one will think that you need help if you stay busy enough.

Your emotional self-awareness is like a muscle—the more you rely on it, the stronger it becomes. The reverse is true and is the reality for the people-pleaser. As they ignore their emotional self-awareness, it starts to atrophy. As you stop caring how you feel, you feel less. You stop knowing what you want. You forget that you want anything, and then you inevitably lower your self-esteem. In its absence, it makes sense to begin seeing yourself through other people's eyes and conflate self-worth with how happy people are with you.

3. You say "yes" when you mean "no."

In your efforts to make other people happy, you do things out of duty instead of genuine desire or interest. It could be doing your friend a favor, loaning your brother money again, or agreeing to work during the weekend. The people-pleaser is like a country whose soldiers lay it under siege. They are like a country whose spies betray it or a soccer player who scores against his team.

In some ways, people-pleasing is a complex phenomenon. The people who people-please the best are often those with a generous attitude toward the world and deep empathy. These traits are valuable for the individual and a culture. A generous person will share even when they have little and will give for the sake of giving. The empathetic person can create genuine trust and is adept at forming bonds. Both these people inspire others to be their best versions by connecting with them on a deeper level. They form the backbone of good communities because they model cooperative social behavior. Empathy has many rewards—it nuances social relationships, morality, and love.

Yet, empathy is not a trait that you can turn off. It is reflexive, instinctual, and automatic. The same way you cannot touch a flame without burning is how an empathetic person cannot encounter someone in distress and fail to feel their pain. The generous cannot see a person in need without wanting to help. Yet, the people-pleaser with a generous and empathetic temperament will reach the ends of their goodwill. They then become people who lean into their inclination to care for others at the cost of themselves, often disassociating their emotions and saying things they do not mean, agreeing to tasks when they mean to say no.

4. Your needs come last.

Because the people-pleaser is busy meeting everyone else's needs, theirs come last or do not even enter the frame. They try to numb their needs or pretend that their needs do not exist, but that never works. In Gary Vaynerchuk's book, he argues that good-natured people can ask for what they want in return for doing good for others, but that is nearly impossible for people-pleasers to do. Asking for what you want is a life skill, but it stands in opposition to everything the people-pleaser believes. They have to break off the compulsion to please in order to demand to have their needs met. The people-pleaser has to have come a long way to even know what they need.

One reason people-pleasers do not notice their people-pleasing nature is that they attach themselves to valuable outlets. They are in it to help, and so they do not ask for what they need. You end up putting in years of arduous work that will never be paid, and you convince yourself that you do not mind. You are always in need, and your emotional tank is always empty. Even with that reality, the people-pleaser can negotiate on behalf of others, but they have difficulties advocating for themselves.

Think of this in terms of business. In a culture based on economic gain, a person's ability to negotiate their pay and status is a personal responsibility. If a person does not ask, they should not expect to receive. Even in business, the economy of giving and pleasing is not seen as a collective good that begs collective responsibility. You can see this principle at work with common sayings like "dog-eat-dog world" or "good guys finish last." Yet, the people-pleaser refuses, so to speak, "to eat what they kill." They fail to be concerned with their own happiness. They do not even recognize that their happiness is their responsibility or that they have such a need.

As a people-pleaser, friends give you compliments like "You are so accommodating!" or "It must be easy to be you—you never need anything!" Your motto is "I am fine," and yet "fine" for you is a permanent estrangement from yourself. Your greatest hope is to be with people who do not abuse your nature, but with such a mentality you never have your needs met unless by accident or by the goodwill of a third party going out of their way to help. Such people are exceedingly rare, and so your needs will always come last.

5. You become resentful because your needs are not met.

We all have wants and needs. There are some needs that you can meet for yourself, and others are met in relationships with other people. A healthy individual can communicate their needs by being assertive and setting boundaries. Otherwise, their needs do not get met. The people-pleaser is incapable of asserting themselves and setting boundaries, and so they are always in want. After a while, they become resentful. When the people-pleaser buckles under the weight of their resentment, it becomes clear to them how much effort they have been expending and how little they have been getting in return. They swear to do better in advocating for themselves and may temporarily break free from whatever claustrophobic situation they are in. That change never lasts unless the root of their people-pleasing is dealt with. But what root is that? What causes people-pleasing behavior?

It might seem like people-pleasing is something someone can "simply stop," and yet, the issue is complicated because the origins are far more complex than may appear at surface level. People-pleasers begin as parent pleasers. They develop the skill to maintain connection and closeness with parents who are inconsistently available to them. Lack of parental attunement is a significant part of what causes people-pleasing. Often, parents of people-pleasers worry too much about their troubles that they cannot tune in to their children's thoughts and feelings. In other cases, they misinterpret or mislabel the child's feelings and signals.

The parents of people-pleasers are often emotionally over-whelmed, leading their children to treat them as though they were fragile. Sometimes, the people-pleaser children play adult roles in relationships with their parents, taking on the care-giving role although they should be the ones receiving care. Eventually, the parent struggles to be emotionally available and connected to their child consistently. The child picks up on it and works to protect their feelings and their parent's feelings to stay connected.

As children, people-pleasers only feel love when they conform to the desires and needs of their parents. Submitting to parental preferences was rewarded, and deviating was met with a measure of displeasure. When such a child asserted themselves and their will was contrary to parental wishes, their parents withheld support, attention, positive time, encouragement, understanding, or recognition. As a result, they felt not just disapproved of, but also rejected and abandoned.

Dependent upon the acceptance of their parents and fearful that it would be withdrawn if they failed to behave right, it was apparent to people-pleaser children what they needed to do. They could either submit to the rules and regulations explicitly and implicitly demanded of them and in so doing receive care, or they could disobey and suffer the consequences. The consequences involved a rupture in the caretaker-child attachment bond, a bond that was already tenuous. Feeling obliged to leave out a chunk of themselves to be secure in their home, the child decided to squash their essential needs.

The people-pleaser child had to renounce the expression of many of their feelings, desires, and needs. They experienced the abdication of self as a necessary sacrifice which they made willingly and with one mind. After all, surrendering a part of who you are is better than feeling forsaken by your caretaker, they figure. To not do whatever was necessary to deal with the danger of parental alienation was to risk guilt, shame, and humiliation. It felt less hazardous to abandon the self than to risk being abandoned by parents.

Over time, the choice between parental abandonment and self-abandonment became imperative. Without any resources to help themselves, the child felt compelled to abandon their budding individualism. The longing for security prompted conformity and compliance, and it prevailed over the desire to be true to self.

It is noteworthy that while the original cause of people-pleasing is the messages, both covert and overt, that people-pleasers get from caretakers, other forces make the situation worse. Perfectionism, for example, has been found to contribute toward people-pleasing behavior. Having learned to put other people first, the people-pleaser with perfectionistic tendencies goes on to perfect the "art," seeking to become the best at making other people happy. The lesson to "comply" rather than be an individual may further be reinforced by being poor, from a minority group, or female.

After a period of self-abandonment, the people-pleaser becomes good at propping their parents up emotionally. She tracks their moods, checking in frequently to make parents proud. She does the best she can not to rock the boat and, in so doing, practices her people-pleasing skills daily. She becomes less interested in exploring her individuality and starts learning about what others expect of her. The child never realizes that her parent's behavior has nothing to do with her.

The people-pleaser carries her behavior into adult relationships, looking to please others and make them happy so that she can be happy. Since it is possible to have people-pleasing behaviors and not know about them, reading about sociotropy helps everyone. Here, you have a mirror against which you can judge your life. Do you see yourself in some of the things discussed in this chapter? Are you uncertain whether you are a people-pleaser and would like to find out for sure?

It is also possible to exhibit people-pleasing tendencies in some relationships and not in others. In one area of life, you may have handed the responsibility for all your decisions to others. To begin the journey of being honest with yourself and with others, you need to know the facts about your situation. They will help you in your self-reflection.

SUMMARY AND ACTIVITY

Because children take everything personally, they believe that if they are being mistreated, it's because they haven't been "good enough." Being good as an adult makes them believe, incorrectly, that they have some control in life. They think that they will be rewarded for their goodness and that it will protect them from harm.

— **MARCIA SIROTA**

Let us recap the things you have learned from this chapter:

Sociotropy or people-pleasing is behavior in which a person considers relationships with others to be more important than their independence. The people-pleaser does everything they can, bending over backward to keep people happy. People-pleasers were once parent-pleasers. The problem with sociotropy is that:

- You cannot please everyone.
- You lose yourself.
- You tie your self-worth to others' opinion of you.
- You cannot speak your mind.
- Your needs stay unmet.
- You become resentful.

Activity: In your journal, summarize the reasons why you think you could be a people-pleaser. How do you think people-pleasing affects you?

2

AM I A PEOPLE-PLEASER?

Understandably, some people find it hard to identify people-pleasing behavior. This chapter will allow you to explore different perspectives to help you look at various areas of your life to determine whether you have people-pleasing behaviors. You will find a test at the end of the chapter that you can take to help you know where to begin your journey to becoming more assertive. To get you started, here are three reasons why being too agreeable does not help to make great relationships:

- People-pleasers, who by default neglect themselves for the sake of others, naturally attract users. You end up in relationships with abusive and lazy partners, friends, and co-workers.
- People-pleasers, because they hide their real

personality—their opinions and feelings—for the sake of being agreeable, end up looking uninteresting to others, which brings challenges in their personal life. You may have difficulties finding a romantic partner, for example.

- Many people are suspicious of those who always agree with everything. People-pleasers always appear disingenuous and challenging to figure out. What is more, because people-pleasers appear bland and neutral, other people have difficulties connecting with them. This gets in the way of meaningful relationships.

People-pleasers often end up hurt and alone in relationships. A common complaint from people-pleasers is that other people do not care about them as much as they care. Do any of these things sound familiar? Do you shudder at the thought of standing your ground? Do you obsess about other people's opinions of you and whether you are doing something that would cause them to dislike you? Do you make choices based on people's opinions because you fear disappointing them? If you answered yes to any of these questions, you likely have people-pleasing tendencies.

It is difficult not to struggle with people-pleasing at some point. As social beings, our nature is to get along with others. We come from a lineage of people whose survival hinged on collaborating with the pack. Back then, when we went hunting in packs and lived in tight-knit tribes, it made sense to want to be similar to everyone else. Yet, there is a fine line between healthy social behavior and experiencing emotional depletion because of sociotropy. Besides becoming emotionally drained, you may find yourself having to compromise your values and principles in order to gain acceptance. As you help other people to get what they want, your well-being and health begin to suffer.

People-pleasing behavior manifests in different ways, but some behaviors are common, including:

1. You are incapable of saying no.

Do you have difficulties turning down requests from friends and family? What about requests from strangers and acquaintances? The person with sociotropy always wants to say no, but they say yes to different demands. Before you know it, you are the go-to person whenever there is a need. From the small things to the big ones, every task is assigned to you. Some people may even think of you as a hero. On the inside, though, you are suffering. While you genuinely want to help others, you know that every "yes" is depleting your resources, yet you fear losing your good reputation and friendships. After all, you are not a selfish person, are you?

2. You avoid making decisions.

Do you have a hard time letting your friends and family know your feelings? Can you not share your opinion in group settings? Are you always leaving others to make your choices? People-pleasers understand that opinions and decisions divide.

However, they feel that it is against their nature to cause a division by speaking up, so they remain silent. Over time, you successfully silence your voice and rob the world of your unique gifts and perspectives.

3. You are dismayed to find someone who does not like you.

The people-pleaser cannot imagine why a person would fail to like them. It seems reasonable that everyone would be impressed with them since they work so hard to please people. Yet, some people will dislike you for reasons outside of your control. Some people-pleasers understand this fact but cannot stop themselves from trying to win over the few holdouts.

4. You are resentful of other people without cause.

This happens when we suppress our needs and feelings over the long term. Do you feel unexplained anger toward your boss, spouse, or close friends? Reflecting on your resentment might reveal some people-pleasing behaviors in those relationships. The anger is your subconscious letting you know that you have neglected yourself for a while as you help others to advance their goals. Resentment is like the check engine light in your car. Please do not ignore it.

5. You are unaware of your limits until you are in too deep.

People-pleasers lack proper boundaries. If you find that you never know where to stop, it could be because you avoid setting limits, as you think they are opposed to a generous spirit. However, a lack of boundaries only allows people greater latitude to intrude into your space. Some requests get more unreasonable with time, and you may not realize it until someone crosses a line. If you take on too much, you might experience passive-aggressive behavior, anxiety, depression, or crying for no reason at all.

6. You have a low opinion of yourself.

Sociotropy is commonly tied to low self-esteem because you draw your self-worth from other people's approval. "I am only worthy to be loved if I give everything to another person," is a common belief connected with people-pleasing. You may come to think that people love you only when you are helpful. You end up relying on their appreciation and praise to feel good about yourself.

7. You accept blame or apologize when you are not at fault.

Are you always ready to say "sorry" whenever something goes wrong? People-pleasing involves a readiness to carry the blame even when you are not at fault. Imagine your boss asked you to order pizza for lunch, but the restaurant mixed the order up. You ordered two gluten-free pizzas, but you did not get them. As a result, three of your co-workers will not be able to eat lunch. The receipt states "gluten-free," making it clear that the mistake was the restaurant's. What do you do? The people-pleaser is likely to apologize repeatedly, feeling horrible and believing that they have fallen out of favor with their co-workers forever.

8. You are not authentic.

People-pleasers have a more challenging time recognizing their feelings. Continually pushing your needs to the side makes it harder for you to recognize and acknowledge them. Eventually, you become unsure about what you want or who you are. You enter a stage where you silence yourself not just to please others, but also because you have no idea who you are. For example, you might not let your partner know they hurt your feelings because "they did not mean it," or "I will hurt their feelings if I say something."

9. You are a giver.

Do you enjoy giving to other people? The people-pleaser does not just give for the sake of giving; they give to be liked. You might find that in some areas, all the good that you do is driven by the desire to be seen and liked. Making sacrifices feeds your sense of self. For the chronic people-pleaser, it might even produce a sense of martyrdom.

10. You have no free time.

Being busy does not mean that you are a people-pleaser. Think keenly about how you spend your free time. After taking care of the essential responsibilities like chores, childcare, and work, what is left of you? Do you get time to relax and to have hobbies? It might be that you use every spare minute you have trying to make other people happy. Try to identify the last time you did something for yourself. Do you have many such moments?

You can be generous without allowing other people to use you. You can be kind without becoming a pushover. You can have a good reputation without selling your soul. That is what you will learn in this book. Do not allow your insecurities and fears to turn you into a slave to other people. You can care for yourself to make sure you have enough love to give others. In such a life, it is true freedom.

People-pleasing never exists in a vacuum. It touches all elements of being. Other than the typical ways people-pleasing shows up, it also interacts with shyness and physical health. Some people-pleasers, for example, think they are too shy to become assertive. They wonder whether their personality has given them the short end of the stick when it comes to assertiveness training.

Shyness is a feeling of discomfort caused by other people, felt more so among strangers or in new situations. It is a feeling of self-consciousness or of concern over what you believe others are thinking. Shyness gets in the way of a person's ability to do or say what they want. It can also get in the way of healthy relationships. It is often linked to low self-esteem and may be a cause of social anxiety.

Shyness often varies in strength. Many people experience mild feelings of discomfort, but they can overcome them. Others feel extreme fear when they are thrust into social situations. Withdrawal from social activities, depression, inhibition, and anxiety can result from shyness. It encompasses a broad spectrum of behaviors. Perceptions of shyness can also be cultural. Some cultures, for example, think of shyness as a negative character trait while others regard it more positively. About 15% of infants are born leaning toward shyness (Rubin & Coplan, 2010). Research has proven a biological difference in the brains of shy people. Yet, the propensity for shyness is also influenced by social experiences. Most shy people, for example, develop the trait because of how they interacted with their parents. This is one of the ways that shyness is similar to people-pleasing—in its development.

Authoritarian or overprotective parents can influence their children toward shyness. Children who are never allowed to experience different childhood situations grow up without the necessary social skills. Children brought up in a warm and caring home often end up being comfortable around other people. Other than the child's home, schools, communities, and neighborhoods also shape a person. The connections made within those networks contribute to their development.

Researchers have looked into the relationship between shyness and sociotropy. In one study, sociotropy was found to predict variance in some aspects of interpersonal concerns through interactive and direct relations with shyness. Another study found that people-pleasing, not shyness, was predictive of how people viewed the participants in situations that involved assertion and initiation of conversations (Bruch, Rivet, Heimberg, Hunt & McIntosh, 1999). Further research found that sociotropy accounted for significant increases in variance when predicting practical and cognitive manifestations of distress connected with simulated conversation and situations where the speaker had to be assertive. The point here is that people-pleasing operates in an additive manner, with shyness affecting interpersonal relations.

When it comes to physical health, people-pleasing also takes its toll. Cory is a 35-year-old single mum to Travis, 11 years old. She works full-time as a receptionist and offers three to four evening meals every week to her father, Bob. Bob is a widower who recently underwent hip replacement surgery. Cory is constantly struggling to balance the demands of housework, her work, her son's homework and sports, and her father's needs. If her friends or relatives are in town, Cory always offers a place for them to stay. She feels uncomfortable with her weight, with her blood pressure and cholesterol seriously high. Cory has a hard time sleeping, and she never has enough time in her day to exercise or even read something she finds enjoyable. Her meals are often delivered or junk food to suit the preferences of others around her. Cory is a people-pleaser, answering the bell to offer companionship and help others. Her example helps illustrate how people-pleasing interacts with physical health.

To help others, many times the people-pleaser suppresses her needs or compromises in the service of stable relationships. Yet, it is crucial to maintain good health and recognize when your good nature is being taken for granted. The people-pleaser is not a stranger to self-neglect. They give the time that they would have used to exercise to others. Like Cory, the people-pleaser cannot make healthy food choices and take the time to relax, risking both their physical health and mental health. Research has found that people-pleasing affects physical health due to the buildup of anger and resentment from a failure to express one's own opinions. You end up becoming more demanding, manipulative, and selfish (Lea Stening Health, 2017).

Constantly repressing one's true feelings causes frustration, low self-esteem, anxiety, and depression, and is often associated with fatigue, sleep deprivation, weight gain, and failing immunity. In Cory's case, while she may be trying to show her father and son that she cares about them, she may also teach her son that women do not have needs and a right to be cared for and heard. If Cory could prioritize time to go for a walk with her son and share activities, she could teach Travis both life skills as well as that everyone in a family should be heard and cared for. It could help her create time to enjoy good food and exercise.

The point here is that when commitments to other people take up a person's free time, there is less opportunity to plan, shop for, and prepare healthy meals, and exercise. Added to these limitations, the people-pleaser may also experience pressure from friends and family, which feeds into their self-destructive behaviors like eating more, drinking more alcohol, or eating only takeout food. Bending to the will of others easily bears other self-destructive habits. No wonder many dieticians are now training in cognitive tehavioral Therapy to help their clients develop different problem-solving techniques and coping mechanisms when managing diet and weight-related issues. While unhealthy eating eventually causes ill-health, it is often the supporting behaviors and relationships around food access, choices, and preparation that worsen the situation.

If you are still unsure whether you have people-pleasing behaviors after reading this chapter, take a piece of paper and pen and complete this test. This people-pleaser test is designed to help you evaluate yourself and clarify areas or relationships where you might need to improve. It comprises 20 questions derived from various research on people-pleasing. Do not overanalyze the questions. The test matches you against an ideal. Bear in mind that it is meant to offer an initial assessment to use as a starting point for self-development. Please reflect on the statementshonestly according to what you really do, think, or feel, rather than what you think is right for this test. No one is there to judge you—only yourself.

		Always	Often	Sometimes	Rarely	Never
1	When I sense someone disagrees with me, I tend to soften my position.					
2	I am conscious of my image.					
3	I can easily set boundaries with everyone.					
4	I intentionally compliment people to seem more likeable.					
5	"Always put others first" is a good motto to live by.					
6	I work overtime to please my colleagues and/or my boss.					
7	I value romantic relationships. I feel incomplete without a relationship.					
8	Conflict makes me anxious so I avoid confrontation.					
9	I am treated like a doormat.					

10	I compare myself to others.					
11	I put other people's feelings before my own.					
12	Whenever my friends complain about something, I tend to agree with them even if I secretly think that they are wrong.					
13	I forgive those who hurt me out of a fear of losing relationships, even when it still hurts.					
14	I only try things I know I can succeed at.					
15	I give more than I take.					
16	I am often stuck doing things I rather not do because I can't say "no."					
17	I love my friends more than they love me.					
18	I copy other people's clothing and behavioral styles.					
19	I don't complain about a bad product or service.					
20	I apologize when I do not have to.					

Each question is worth five points. Use the following key to score yourself and multiply the number of correct answers by five to get your score. If your answer does not match those provided, the score for that question is zero.

Q1—Rarely, **Q2**—Sometimes, **Q3**—Always, **Q4**—Sometimes, **Q5**—Never, **Q6**—Rarely, **Q7**—Never, **Q8**—Rarely, **Q9**—Never, **Q10**—Rarely, **Q11**—Rarely, **Q12**—Never, **Q13**—Never, **Q14**—Sometimes, **Q15**—Sometimes, **Q16**—Never, **Q17**—Never, **Q18**—Rarely, **Q19**—Never, **Q20**—Never

Less than 20 points

You are incredibly dependent on the way other people think about you. If someone mistreats you or is condescending toward you, you automatically shoulder the blame. You tend to get caught up in an unproductive cycle of self-blame and could feel worn out, anxious, and depressed. There are many problems with this approach. Your chronic people-pleasing will not get you results because you will end up being used by manipulative people, and you will not connect with healthy people because you won't feel like they know the real you. In this book, you will find strategies to help you in assertiveness training. Cognitive behavioral therapy might also help you change your thinking patterns to change the way you act and feel.

20–39 points

While you are not as bad a people-pleaser as you could be, you sacrifice a lot. You may be very assertive with some people in your life while getting taken advantage of by other people. You will likely have a hard time asserting yourself with some of the people you value most—your children, spouse, or some of your family members. You are draining your energy and feel resentful. Learning to set boundaries and to say "no" will be helpful to you.

40–69 points

You are a considerate and warm person without being desperate or needy. You believe that to care for the needs of others, your needs should first be met. There are many times that you give more than you take, and there are even more times that you withhold your opinions in service of diplomacy. In general, you are your own best friend, and you care for others as energy and time permit.

70–100 points

You think independently and have a healthy sense of your worth. You handle criticism well, either by treating it as helpful feedback or by dismissing it when it does not apply to you. This helps you to go after your goals and to treat your failures as an opportunity to learn. You are not primarily concerned with diplomacy, and some people resent you for not being as considerate or sensitive as they would like you to be.

SUMMARY AND ACTIVITY

Sometimes you cannot hear your body because all you hear is the expectations of others.

— ANN VOSKAMP

From this chapter, you have learned that people-pleasing is not just bad for your mental well-being, it also affects your physical health. Before you know it, you are overweight, unhappy with your food choices, and constantly feeling fatigued—you struggle with anxiety and are constantly overwhelmed by other people's demands on you. People-pleasing causes you to constantly feel tired and develop other physical complications because you are not getting enough rest.

You have also learned common behaviors of people-pleasers, including:

- Inability to say "no."
- Indecisiveness
- Inability to handle other people's bad opinions
- Unexplained resentment
- Ignorance of one's limits
- Low self-esteem

- Shouldering underserved blame
- Inauthenticity
- Giving even when it hurts
- Busyness

Activity: Take a moment to consider your results from the test. How well are you doing? Are you able to identify areas of improvement? Are you willing to do better? In a journal, write down what your ideal life would look like if you were not people-pleasing. Are you able to identify relationships or inter-actions that trigger your people-pleasing behaviors?

3

THE EFFECTS OF PEOPLE-PLEASING

The people-pleaser imagines themselves to be one of the nice people—kind and helpful. They get thrilled by brightening someone's day. They strive for harmony and peace in their relationships. They always "take one for the team," because self-sacrifice is in their nature. Their typical response to any perceived request or need is yes.

Yes. I will do it.
Yes. I will happily join you... help you... care for you...
Yes. You are right.

Often, this strategy works well, making the people-pleaser feel good for helping others. Yet, the emotion lurking in the background is increasing with every good deed. Your approach to relationships crosses a line—you are not just helpful, you take on responsibility for other people's reactions and feelings. It is vital to have a disclaimer here. It is a good thing to desire connection with other people and to respond to their needs. You do not have to give that up. The challenge is to develop personal strength—a little backbone—that will allow you to say "no" when it counts. The effects of people-pleasing tend to be felt in the long term.

The person with sociotropy takes on too much. It does not seem okay to disappoint anyone, so they say yes to more commitments and tasks than they can handle, leading to being overworked. What is more, people-pleasing will not allow your light to shine. You end up performing at less than your best because you are always worried about the social consequences of being better than others. You worry that if you outperform someone else, they will feel envious or hurt, and could even become hostile toward you. Research has found that sociotropy is a reliable predictor of such discomfort in outperformance (Sato, McCann & Ferguson-Isaac, 2004).

The more you people-please, the more you get used to caving in to social pressure. The people-pleaser is not interested in making waves. You find it tough to live by your principles when you are under pressure. For example, you might want to eat less because you are concerned about your weight, but you decide to match what others around you eat. The same pattern could be true even with things like drinking alcohol, smoking, and drug use. People-pleasing could even cross the line into moral lapses, as shown in research regarding obedience to authority (Milgram, 2017). If you are determined to please someone who is pressuring you, the voice of your conscience becomes drowned out. This means that often, your yes will come with a bitter aftertaste.

Yes ... but I will not be happy about it.
Yes ... but only because I cannot say "no."
Yes ... although I think you should not do it that way.

Sociotropy is also tied to depression. It is one of the different interpersonal styles that increase the risk of depressive symptoms. Internally, you create problems for yourself when you agree to something even though you are not entirely sold on it. You lose touch with the deeper parts of yourself because your routine is accommodating everyone else's preferences. One of the many problems this can create is body-image issues. One research study involving 362 people between 18 and 29 years found that sociotropy interacts with body-image factors. The research looked into eating disorder behaviors and attitudes, physical activity, and body shape satisfaction. Both men and women with sociotropy were found to have a degree of eating disorders.

The research found that both men and women with people-pleasing behavior had less dietary restraint. They had a higher dissatisfaction with their body shape and were concerned about their weight, shape, and eating behaviors. These participants scored within the body-shape questionnaire's clinical range, suggesting that their problems were more perception-related than reality (Friedman & Whisman, 1998). Other research shows that people high in sociotropy engage more frequently in emotional eating (Palmer, 2005). People-pleasers do not believe that their bodies warrant the approval they are looking for, and so they engage in behaviors to change their bodies.

People-pleasing affects relationships as well. Struggling to ask for help and fear of abandonment could seem like two character traits that are not connected, but they share a common thread. Most people who identify with these behaviors have a similar attachment style that is characterized by insecurity and is familiar with people-pleasers—the insecure attachment style.

An insecure attachment style is an approach to relationships characterized by uncertainty or fear. It is one of several attachment styles that can make it hard for people to make deep, intimate, and emotional connections with a partner or loved ones. A person with an insecure attachment style generally feels anxious about relationships. They are unsure whether the other person can meet their desires or needs. Typically, they expect that the person they are in a relationship with will leave them or hurt them somehow. The term "insecure attachment" is an umbrella term for describing other attachment styles that are not secure. Three types of attachment styles fall under this term, including:

Anxious attachment

An anxious attachment style is characterized by insecurity in relationships. The person becomes preoccupied with worries and is clingy. In a parent-child relationship, the child is hyper-aware of subtle shifts in their parent's mood. In romantic relationships, you imagine that your partner's mood changes mean that they are no longer interested in you. You are always seeking reassurance from them. Reassurance-seeking behaviors could be anything from repetitive calling to threatening to break up. The anxiously attached person always panics when they do not hear from their partner and readily sacrifices their needs for the relationship.

Avoidant attachment

Dismissive behaviors characterize the avoidant attachment style. These people avoid intimacy and emotional closeness. They struggle with asking for help. People with this attachment style are used to neglectful caregivers. As children, the caregiver would discourage them from crying or having needs, which made them feel rejected and unseen. The caregiver's neglectful approach causes the child to suppress their need for emotional comfort and develop an auto-regulating system. The system makes it hard to have a connected and mutual experience of intimacy.

As adults, people who resonate with this style tend to rely on themselves mostly. They develop an inflated sense of self that covers their deep fears of abandonment. They are often career-oriented, minimizing the importance of relationships. When they get into relationships, they avoid tending to their friends' or partners' needs and unconsciously create a distance that protects them from harm. They end up focusing on flaws or spending little physical time with their loved ones, which helps them block out too much intimacy. These people struggle to be vulnerable and to express their needs and inner world to other people.

Fearful-avoidant attachment

This attachment style is also known as a disorganized attachment style. Volatile and unpredictable behaviors characterize it. Research suggests that these people do not have strong coping strategies, and they struggle to handle relationship problems. People with this attachment style have a strong desire for closeness and connection, but they do not trust it. They are hypersensitive to anything that looks like a betrayal of trust which means that they will sabotage relationships quickly if the trust wound is activated. They tend to overthink what could go wrong in their relationships.

Attachment styles are typically developed in childhood based on caregiver-child relationships. They are essentially a reflection of how you were emotionally cared for—or denied care—as a child. People with insecure attachment styles usually lacked reliability, consistency, safety, and support as children. The majority of people-pleasers have an insecure attachment style. The following is a list of behaviors in childhood that suggest the formation of insecure attachment and how they manifest in adulthood:

In childhood

- Clinginess to the caregiver
- Actively avoiding the caregiver
- Frequent inconsolable crying
- Repressing or hiding emotions
- Getting panicked when a parent leaves
- Seeming independent while secretly craving attention
- Poor emotional regulation
- Fear of exploration

In adulthood

- Difficulties asking for help
- Low self-esteem
- Pushing others away
- Fear of abandonment
- Clinginess
- Resistance to intimacy
- A constant need for reassurance
- Jealousy of a partner's independence

If the insecure attachment style is not resolved, it plays out in adulthood, haunting every one of your relationships. Generally, being insecure as a child is the same as insecurity as an adult in terms of anxiety levels. For example, children who learn early on that they cannot rely on their parents may struggle to rely on their partner as adults. Regardless of the behavior of the partner, the person with an insecure attachment will feel insecure. This spirals into poor emotional regulation, anxiety, and depression.

A study involving 122 men and 133 women found that while there is a positive correlation between people-pleasing and solitude, the independence of solitude causes the people-pleaser to become anxious (Sato & McCann, 1998). People rated high on sociotropy were anxious in situations involving physical danger, social evaluation, and ambiguous situations. Anxiety in daily routines was also found to be related to sociotropy. It follows that anything that would trigger anxiety could worsen people-pleasing behaviors such as:

Health issues

An upsetting diagnosis such as a chronic illness could make anxiety worse. This is a powerful trigger because of the immediate feelings it produces. The people-pleaser forgets to be proactive in managing their health issues and becomes obsessed with how little time they imagine themselves to have, causing them to go on a rampage to help everyone. Certain prescription medications could also trigger anxiety symptoms. Medicines like birth control pills, weight loss medications, and congestion medications have ingredients that increase unease. They could set off a series of events in your body and mind that could increase restlessness. Caffeine could also worsen people-pleasing tendencies because of its effect on social anxiety.

Skipping meals

Whenever you miss a meal, there is a drop in your blood sugar level. This could cause a rumbling tummy, jittery hands, and anxiety that worsens people-pleasing behaviors. Eating a balanced meal serves many roles. It supplies you with essential nutrients and energy, and food inevitably affects your mood.

Negative thinking

Your mind controls your body. When you are frustrated or upset, the things you say to yourself, for example, could trigger anxiety. If you use any negative words when describing yourself in your brain, learning to refocus your feelings and language will be helpful. Negative thinking feeds your low self-worth and continues the people-pleasing cycle. If you are in a room full of strangers, for example, your brain might begin to look for ways to keep you safe. You might find that you have no tolerance for small talk, and so you busy yourself trying to make everyone like you through, perhaps, acts of service.

Conflict

People-pleasers dislike conflict. Arguments, disagreements, and relationship problems can cause them to be anxious. The person with sociotropy has done everything they can think of to avoid getting into a conflict. When they do find themselves in one, they spiral. This ends up triggering more people-pleasing behavior. The people-pleaser hopes that such behavior would get them out of trouble. The conflict does not even need to be huge for sociotropy to be triggered. Daily stressors like missing your train or traffic jams can cause the people-pleaser to work harder to please since they do not like to see other people in distress.

Being pleasant should not involve waiting for other people to approve of you, a debilitating desire to be liked, or the hope for unconditional love. You are worthy as you are. You are loved as you are. Yet, getting to the place where you appreciate these facts is a long journey for someone who has been people-pleasing for a long time. You have likely forgotten the most important person—yourself. It would be best if you learned that you could be pleasant without sacrificing your needs. It would help if you learned to like yourself, approve of yourself, and create the happiness you crave. Your journey will take you to a place where you can share yourself fully with the world. You will learn that it does not matter if some people do not like you. The people who like you and support you as you are will be the ones who matter. You can learn to give yourself unconditional love.

You do not get here by chance, though. You have to reflect on your journey and face some things that you may have found difficult to create better habits. Healing from your past will help you create a present you enjoy and work toward a future you are excited about. As you reflect on your people-pleasing tendencies, you can learn a lot about who you are and how to improve. You will begin to embrace that life is about give and take—serve and be served. As a people-pleaser, you give, give, and then give some more. You believe that you need nothing in return, but the truth is that you deserve to receive.

In self-reflection, you will uncover the relationships in your life that take too much and give you nothing in return. There needs to be balance. Admittedly, that balance is not always perfect—it ebbs and flows—but you cannot be the only one always giving. You need to learn to love yourself. This is not easy because you carry many years of people-pleasing and belief systems that affect the way you see yourself. It takes time to become assertive, and it starts with openness to learning. To start working on being assertive, you will need to be honest with yourself. Look at the areas where you struggle to love yourself, choose what you want to change, and actively work through those areas. This book exists to help you do that. It will demand that you change behaviors and beliefs that do not serve you and learn to view yourself from another perspective.

As a form of assurance, people who matter will always be at your side, more so when you are vulnerable and open in sharing who you are. It will take you time to get there, but every aspect of your life will thank you for the effort. The people who do not accept you entirely are not for you. Once you accept yourself and learn to share yourself fully, you will attract the right people. The point here is, to be more assertive you will need a change in mindset. You will understand what you are responsible for and what is not your responsibility, set boundaries, stand by them, and protect yourself from users.

Without reflection, we go blindly on our way, creating more unintended consequences, and failing to achieve anything useful.

— MARGARET J. WHEATLEY

SUMMARY AND ACTIVITY

From this chapter, you have learned that taking on the burden of other people's expectations, judgments, and responsibilities is not just bad for you, it is also terrible for other people in your life and for your relationships with them. You become unable to take responsibility for your actions if you are constantly trying to please them. You have learned that people-pleasing affects your physical health and have explored different factors that can trigger people-pleasing in you. You know the importance of self-reflection to your self-development journey.

Activity: Create a safe space in your house to reflect. Remember that you desire to grow every day. In this space, do not shame your past self or judge your behavior. You process your thoughts and change your perspective in order to move forward, knowing that you did the best possible. Make sure that the space is comfortable and private. You can journal from that space. Read the section on triggers and identify things that trigger you to people-please. What situations or activities make you anxious? Be honest with yourself, but explore your inner world patiently. Identify what in your past still affects you today and make note of it.

4

THE ASSERTIVE YOU

It is understandable that when you grow up as a people-pleaser, you grow up with a fully formed program that to be loved, you have to comply with others' demands and wishes. People-pleasers are not able to validate themselves, and so they rely on others to affirm them. Not having developed a sense of inherent worth, they strive to become lovable by taking the form dictated by others. As an adult, your habit of disavowing your needs is so well-established that it gets repeated automatically. Allowing others to use you alleviates your social anxieties and brings a level of security. If you are ever going to re-write your inappropriate childhood script and become a better version of yourself, you have to get in touch with and express your true self. That is the path to a sense of well-being and peace of mind.

How then do you disencumber yourself of your self-effacing, life-denying pattern, or at least learn to control it? The short answer is that you have to do it gradually and with a lot of effort. After all, people-pleasing patterns are deeply ingrained in you and are associated with the only kind of acceptance you have ever known. Early adaptation programs that a child saw as tied to survival are always tricky to uproot. They present a difficult challenge because people-pleasing is a type of relationship addiction. Like any other addiction, you need patience, discipline, fortitude, and restraint to overcome it.

To learn to be more self-validating, you have to pick up other skills like self-awareness and assertiveness. You have to anticipate feelings of nervousness, hesitancy, ambivalence, and guilt as you try to work through your issues. To a certain degree, the feelings will show up nearly every time you act in a self-interested manner. Here, you will find out how to acknowledge these feelings as they come up, speak to the child within who bears the doubt, and gently reassure yourself that it is within your rights to assert your needs and refuse demands that feel excessive or unfair. Over and over, you will need to repeat the new and revised message that your desires and wants are important and legitimate and that it is safe to hold onto them even when they are not the same as everyone else's. This is the essence of assertiveness training.

Patricia's Story

Before delving into assertiveness, take a moment to think about this story:

Whenever Patricia goes out on a date, her chief worry is always, "How much does he like me?" She never remembers to ask herself whether or not she likes him. On the date, she doesn't just try to have a good time but focuses on pleasing him. She goes so far as trying to figure out what he likes and adopts those preferences. If she says something and her date disagrees, she backpedals and changes her opinion. No matter what restaurant they go to, she has the same opinion of it as he does. She is not aware that she is trying to please him. That is how things turn out. It works in the short term, making a man want to meet her more frequently, but it backfires in the long term. She often comes across as subdued and bland. The real Patricia is never there.

When her friends do something Patricia does not appreciate, she becomes confused and fuzzy and changes the subject, which helps her to hide her annoyance. Patricia even manages to convince herself that she is okay with the offense. This often means that she feels distant from her friends because her concerns are never addressed. Patricia has been seeing Joe for a few months. One day he asked her to be more outgoing with his family. Patricia immediately felt terrible and tried to give Joe his desire. She never even thought about the reasonableness of his demands. She never tried to identify the genuine concern for Joe and did not even consider the possibility that Joe's demands wanted her to be a certain way. She only thought: "How do I comply with his request? How do I make sure he is not upset with me?" Yet, Patricia did not see it as a request but a demand. Such has been her pattern. She expects others to run and control her life. What could Patricia have done differently? What is assertiveness?

Assertiveness is about having a firm knowledge of what you desire, think, and feel instead of being influenced by others' opinions, feelings, and needs. It is part of being autonomous. It includes exerting power to get what you want, protect yourself, stand up for your beliefs and speak your mind. It could mean exerting power to care for others or to do what you believe is right in a certain situation. Assertiveness does not mean that you are judgmental, aggressive, controlling, or extreme. It naturally integrates with collaboration so that you are open to others' opinions and needs without having to give up yours.

Imagine if Patricia explored her people-pleasing and found out what causes her to "merge" with other people instead of caring for herself. She might find that the part that drives such a response was a protector who was frightened that other people would not love her without sociotropy. Suppose in her exploration, Patricia remembered her mother and their home as well as demands that things go her mother's way. Patricia's mother would be distant and withholding if Patricia did not go along with her wishes, and when she obliged, she would receive the love she craved. Patricia finds that from those experiences, she learned that the only way to get love was to let her mother control her life. As she works on herself, Patricia connects with her inner child and explains that she no longer depends on her mother's love. She reaffirms that she is now a grown woman who has found her place in the world. She asserts that her friends care for her even when she is not going out of her way to please them.

Patricia was unsure where she stood with one friend, but she reassured herself that she did not need to win them all over. She would practice asserting herself with her friends. She started to bring up the issues that were bothering her. They responded well, and her connections with them became deeper. She started to know herself and was enjoying personal power that she never had before. Then she wondered whether Joe would still love her even if she did not agree to everything he wanted. She thought about Joe's request for her to be outgoing with his family and realized that while she could improve, Joe abandoned her at family functions. He did not help her to connect with his family. She asked him to spend more time with her when they met up with his family to help her get comfortable.

Joe was not happy about the request because he wanted to do "guy things" with the men in his family. This allowed Patricia to practice standing up for herself. She assured Joe that he could spend all the time he needed with the men after she felt comfortable with his family. He agreed. Patricia continued asserting herself in other ways with Joe and was surprised to find that not only did Joe not pull away, but their relationship improved. Assertiveness, even in communication, is healthy. Communication problems come up when you become too passive or too aggressive. Neither aggressive nor passive communication passes your message along or gets your needs met.

Assertiveness is inevitably tied to individualism and independence. The dictionary defines individualism as a person's tendency to act without referring to others, more so in their mode of thought, style, and fashion. Individualism is also a moral stance or social outlook that promotes self-reliance and independence in opposition to interfering with other people's choices. Simply put, individualism refers to the ways people define themselves and set their goals. It gives priority to the goals of the individual as opposed to the societal or group goals. Individualists define their own identities according to their attributes, values, and behaviors.

On the other hand, independence is the ability to self-govern—to not owe your life or livelihood to a group or another person. Other people do not control an independent person. They can direct their affairs freely.

In all types of relationships, people-pleasers invest too much of themselves into maintaining the relationship that they forget that they are an individual. Such over-investment becomes worse in romantic relationships. The point of this section is to help you balance your identity when relating with other people. Maintaining individuality is necessary for any relationship to be long-lasting and healthy. Equal efforts need to be put into attending to yourself as you put in making the relationship work. You have to set boundaries to help you guard against being overwhelmed by other people's demands.

Before you set boundaries, you have to know who you are. Answer the following questions:

- What is essential for me?
- What do I need?
- What feelings and thoughts are worth protecting?
- What are my values?
- What traditions or hobbies do I want to keep?
- Which friendships do I want to maintain?

A healthy relationship is one where people feel connected while keeping a strong sense of independence and individuality within the relationship. You do not need to love the same things as the person you are in a relationship with. You need to respect the differences you both have. This is true for all types of relationships, but the danger of losing oneself is typically more pronounced in a romantic relationship. Issues around control and power do not assume much importance in a healthy relationship. This is not to suggest that such a relationship lacks conflict, but that partners deal with conflict fairly. A healthy relationship consists of:

- Trust, friendship, and mutual respect
- Room to maintain and express your individuality
- Ways to ensure safety for both partners and increase their sense of vulnerability and intimacy
- Comfortable boundaries for both partners
- Mutual sharing and occasional trade-offs and sacrifices for the other

One of the things that the people-pleaser lacks is self-awareness. Everyone has a basic idea of what self-awareness is, but few people know where it comes from, its precursors and why it is necessary. Self-awareness theory answers these questions. Self-awareness is the ability to view yourself objectively and clearly through introspection and reflection. It is impossible to be fully objective about yourself, but you can have a high level of self-awareness. Self-awareness exists on a spectrum. The self-awareness theory comes from the idea that your identity is not your thoughts. You are the entity that observes your thoughts (Duval & Wicklund, 1972).

We can go for long periods without thinking much about our inner self, merely feeling, thinking, and acting as we would. In self-evaluation, though, you focus on your inner self. You find out whether you feel, think, and act as you should, according to your values and standards. You compare your behavior and your reality against your ideals. People-pleasers, who have forgotten who they are and what they believe in, need to self-evaluate to begin getting in touch with who they are. Self-awareness helps the people-pleaser:

- To become more proactive. It boosts their acceptance of themselves and encourages positive self-development (Sutton, 2016)
- To see things from other perspectives, practice self-control, work productively and creatively, and experience a sense of pride from their work, contributing to increased self-esteem (Silvia & O'Brien, 2004)
- To make better decisions (Ridley, Schutz, Glanz & Weinstein, 1992)

But what does self-awareness look like in real life?

Bob struggles to create the quarterly report at work, frequently producing low-quality results. He notices that he falls short of his standards and evaluates how he can get better. Bob asks himself what about the report is difficult for him and realizes that his struggle is with the actual writing, rather than doing the work that goes into the report. To fix the problem, he decides to take a writing course and have a colleague review his report before submitting it. He further creates a reusable template for future reports to ensure he does not leave anything out.

Monique has been having problems with her boyfriend, Luis. She thinks Luis is taking her for granted. He does not show enough affection, and they often fight about it. She realizes that she may be part of the problem and, in reflecting, finds that she does not appreciate Luis. She overlooks the things he does around the house to help her. Monique considers her thoughts whenever she feels unappreciated and noticed that she typically assumes the worst—that Luis denies her attention on purpose. She spent time talking with Luis about what they could do better, and they started working on their relationship.

These two stories provide examples of self-awareness at work and its benefits to those who tap into it. Bob might have kept turning in subpar work without self-awareness, and Monique could have stayed in an unsatisfying relationship. These stories are everywhere. Now that you have clear examples of self-awareness, you are probably wondering how to do it. What do you do to practice self-awareness?

To practice self-awareness, you have to start with the basics. You have to get in touch with your values. There is a human drive in all of us to create value, to regard groups, people, objects, and ideas as worthy of time, energy, interest, appreciation, effort, and if the situation calls for it, sacrifice. The experience and creation of value give life its purpose and meaning. Some experts have called this ability a core value. People who are in touch with their core values live a vibrant and rich life. Those people who are not in touch with their core values, like the people-pleasers, experience unnecessary pain in life. Experiencing value gives you a heightened sense of vitality and wellbeing.

You feel alive when you look at a sunset, connect with a loved one, feel genuine compassion, appreciate a creative piece of artwork, or are committed to a cause. Creating value increases your capacity to learn, grow, appreciate, and improve. The more you value your experience, the more meaningful your life becomes, and the less you rely on other people to define you. When we act according to our deepest values, we feel authentic. When we violate our values, we feel shame and guilt—life loses meaning. The people-pleaser has not lost their ability to create value—no one does—they have lost touch with their values. The first step to identifying your core values is to find out the most important thing about you as a person.

What your core values are is not a simple question for a person with sociotropy to answer because there are many essential things and people-pleasing tendencies that blur their view of those things. The question is hard enough for an autonomous individual, how much more for a people-pleaser? For example, when most people are asked this question, they say, "I am loyal, honest, and a hard worker." While these qualities are important, they tend to be of equal value. Core values are more important than anything else.

There are many ways to go about deciding what is most important to you, but this book deals only with the quickest way.

Imagine that you have children and they are grown—what do you want them to feel when they think about you?

1. My parents were loyal, hardworking, and honest (you can replace this with what initially seems like the most important thing about you). I am not sure they loved us, but they were always hardworking and honest.
2. My parents were human. They made mistakes, but I can never doubt their love for us. They wanted the best for us.

Most people choose the second option because love, kindness, and compassion for the people they care about are the most important values. Research shows that people regret that they have not been more compassionate, loving, and kind to their loved ones (Steiner, 2019). If someone close to you passed on, you got a glimpse of that regret. Grievers often wonder whether their relationships with their loved ones were close. "Did they know how much I cared for them? Did I express how important they were to me?" they often wonder. On your deathbed, you will not fret about whether your loved ones thought you were right in a fight, for example. You will worry about the things you value most.

The rewards for staying true to your core values are conviction, authenticity, long-term wellbeing, and freedom from people-pleasing. The reminders for violating your values include feeling inadequate, regret, shame, anxiety, guilt, and feeling unlovable. To find out what you most value then, you have to consult your resentment. You have to face the negative feelings you experience due to your people-pleasing tendencies and ask yourself what the message is in them before letting go of those feelings and doing better in future interactions. You have to do this constantly because the only reliable way to sustain a sense of authenticity is through being true to your deepest values—true to yourself, if you please.

How, then, do you define your values?

To answer this question well, we have to start by defining "values." Your values are the things you believe to be important in the way you work and live. They should determine what you prioritize and are the measures you use to determine how well your life is turning out. When your actions and how you behave match your values, life is good—you are content and satisfied. When they do not align, as is the case for people-pleasers, things feel wrong. This is why it is crucial to make a conscious effort to identify your values. Values exist whether or not you recognize them. Life will become easier when you acknowledge yours and make decisions and plans that honor your values.

If you value family, for example, yet spend 70 hours every week at work, you will feel internal conflict and stress. If you do not value competition and your workplace is highly competitive, will you be satisfied with your job? In situations like these, understanding your values helps. That way, you can use them to make decisions about your life. You can decide the kind of job to pursue, whether or not to take a promotion, whether to start a business, the friends you want to hang around, and so forth. Take time to understand your life's real priorities, and you will have set yourself in the right direction toward overcoming people-pleasing.

As a rule of thumb, values are usually stable, but they do not have to be strict boundaries. As you move through life, they may change. For instance, when you begin your career, you may measure success by status and money, but when your family grows, you may value work-life balance more. In this example, as your definition of success changes, your core values change as well. This is why you need to adopt getting in touch with your values as a lifelong exercise. You should revisit it continuously, more so if you start feeling unbalanced. As you perform the following exercise, remember that values you may have had in the past may be different now.

1. Identify the times you were happiest.

Find examples in your life and your career when you felt the most content. Having examples in the two areas will balance your answers. What were you doing then? Were you alone or with others? If others, who? What factors contributed to your contentment?

2. Identify the times you felt most proud.

Why were you proud? Did other people share your pride? What factors contributed to the feelings of pride?

3. Find the times you were most fulfilled.

What desire or need was met? How did the experience give you a sense of meaning, and why? What other factors played a role in your feelings of satisfaction?

4. Determine your core values based on the experiences in 1, 2, and 3.

Why was each experience truly memorable and important? You can use the following list of shared values as a springboard. Aim for the ten most important values. As you work through the exercise, some may naturally combine. For example, community, generosity, and philanthropy may connect to become "service to others." This list is not exhaustive. You can use other adjectives that you find to be a better fit.

Accountability	Positivity	Practicality	Belonging
Perfection	Adventurousness	Ambition	Fluency
Excellence	Altruism	Faith	Boldness
Expertise	Exploration	Prudence	Focus
Accuracy	Expressiveness	Balance	Freedom
Excitement	Professionalism	Fidelity	Resourcefulness
Piety	Preparedness	Reliability	Self-control
Achievement	Fairness	Fitness	Fun
Restraint	Elegance	Patriotism	Originality
Security	Diversity	Honesty	Uniqueness
Generosity	Creativity	Loyalty	Tolerance
Goodness	Loyalty	Courtesy	Truth-seeking
Equality	Empathy	Efficiency	Success

5. Prioritize your values

You will likely find this step to be the most difficult because you have to do further self-reflection. It is also the most vital step because you will have to choose between solutions that meet different needs and satisfy different values when decision-making. In your list of values, pick any two and ask yourself, "If

I could satisfy one of these, which one would I pick?" It might help you to visualize a specific situation where you would have to make a choice. For instance, if you compare stability and service, imagine deciding between selling your house to move to another country to do foreign aid work or keeping your home and volunteering in a charity close to you. Work through the list by comparing each value with another until you have the correct order.

Keep your list handy. Throughout this book, you will need to refer to it. You will also need your list when making decisions. Make sure that your top-priority values fit with your life and where you imagine being in the future. Do your values make you feel good? Are you proud of them? Would you comfortably tell them to people you admire and respect? Do your values represent things you would support even if you were in the minority because of them?

When you factor in your values during decision-making, you are sure to keep your integrity and approach decisions with clarity and confidence. You will also know that your choice is best for your current and future satisfaction and happiness. Remember that making value-based choices will not always be easy, but it will prove to be a lot less complicated as you become more assertive.

While at it, you will need to consider how you act and how it interacts with what you believe about yourself. Research shows that most people have given no thought to what drives their daily behavior. Often referred to as "motive," the driver for our behavior is based on beliefs that we have about ourselves—these self-beliefs shape the direction and the intensity of our actions. They determine what we do, how we go about it, and the lens we use to view our accomplishments in the world. Self-beliefs are so powerful that they strongly influence the careers we choose, our relationships, and ultimately what we do or refuse to do in life. Ironically, if you picked a person at random on the street and asked them to name the self-beliefs that influence them most, they would not know where to start. Beliefs are implicit, and so they operate unconsciously and automatically.

Often, when people hear the subject of self-beliefs for the first time, they assume it has something to do with religion, but self-beliefs are not religious, secular, or even political. For example, self-beliefs do not include food preferences or whether you prefer reading to gain knowledge instead of watching videos. They are guiding principles and assessments that we make about outcomes we expect from our capabilities. In bringing these beliefs to the conscious mind, you can take steps to harness their power and influence. You can change the things that you have come to believe about yourself that you no longer want.

The most dominant belief is our assessment of how much control we have over our future and fate. The degree to which you believe you have control over how your life turns out dictates whether you pursue goals for external reasons (as is the case in people-pleasing) or satisfy an inner psychological striving emanating from the core self—people whose focus is external feel that they cannot control their destiny. Diminished beliefs about control result in ascribing accomplishments and life events to circumstances or luck. The people-pleaser cannot and will not influence what happens. They may start to believe themselves stuck in a workplace they do not like because of "poor market conditions." Frequently, they will not look for challenges and will avoid having personal goals. Instead, they will settle for the status quo. Conversely, if you have strong beliefs and feel that you are in command of your world, the internal focus will be a catalyst for personal growth. You take responsibility for your actions and become accountable for your failures or successes.

Other than beliefs about control, self-beliefs also surround competency. Beliefs about your overall ability to achieve an outcome you desire will determine how much of yourself you give to the task. These beliefs affect both the big decisions in life, like getting married as well as the small choices, such as installing computer software. Of course, your sources of competency appraisals will be different. Sometimes you judge your competency based on how you performed in the past, while other times, you focus on the current challenge. People tend to appraise their competence levels upon presumed competency beliefs rather than the actual ability and knowledge. The people-pleaser judges their competency based on other people's perception of them.

Finally, self-beliefs touch on the value associated with different task outcomes. If a task has a low-value outcome, people invest less of themselves. If you find yourself unwilling to exert effort toward a particular moral action, it could be that you believe that the value is not worth it. James Allen is credited with saying that a man is his thoughts. The idea behind this is that what you believe determines what you become. You see what you look for and attract what you are. Bruce Lee put it this way: "You will never get more than you think you can get." What you truly and deeply believe to be true about yourself and what your future holds is what will play out.

What do you believe? If you always let others do your thinking, you will never become who you want to be. The fact is, if you have been people-pleasing for long, it is easier to let other people do your thinking. It is convenient. If other people call the shots and things do not work, it is not your fault: it is theirs. By becoming assertive, you will become willing to take full responsibility for your life. You will start to work toward what you truly want.

A Visualization Technique

You probably think that being assertive sounds lovely, but are wondering what it looks like. What happens when you make more self-oriented choices? What would your life look like if you said "no" when you wanted to say "no"? In visualizing your life without people-pleasing, you will have something more authentic to work toward. Visualization is more than having a mental picture of what you hope for. It is more than meditation and can serve you in your daily life in practical ways. The reason why visualization techniques work so well is that when we focus our minds, we create.

Through visualization and seeing something in your "mind's eye," you activate the same neural pathways in the brain as if you were experiencing whatever you are visualizing. This means that you are programming your mind whenever you visualize things, like seeing yourself making a self-oriented decision in your future. You are setting your subconscious mind up to believe that you can and will make those moments a reality in your future life. In that sense, visualization is powerful. The good thing about it is that you cannot get it wrong. However, some things can help you to get the best possible results from the visualization technique provided later in this chapter:

1. Do not overthink things.

Everyone has a different experience with visualization. Some people find it more challenging than expected, while others find it easier than they thought it would be. Either way, when visualizing, do not overthink it. For example, if you are trying to picture a tree in your mind, you might start trying to get the right kind of tree. Yet, when you start to think that way, you are overthinking. The key to perfecting your visualization technique is to put little to no mental effort into the process. The more you can let the experiences or images come to you instead of seeking them out, the more beneficial visualization will be.

2. Use all your senses.

Visualization is not simply creating a mental picture. You will get the best results from the practice if you use your sense of touch, smell, taste, sound, and sight. Using all your senses and adding as many details as possible to what you are picturing will give you a more vivid experience. When visualizing, try to notice any smells, sounds, and tastes if you can. The more details you experience, the greater the effect of your visualization on your body and mind.

3. Try not to judge yourself if you get distracted.

When you start the visualization technique, you may find that your mind wanders off. Whether you find yourself dwelling on your to-do list or thinking of a problem at work, remember that it is normal for the untrained mind to wander. Try not to judge yourself. Instead, bring back your awareness to your visualization practice. Take a deep breath and get back to the visualization itself.

4. Stay relaxed.

It is essential to feel relaxed as you visualize. When you are relaxed, you are in an open stare. The feelings and imagery you are trying to conjure in your practice will come naturally, and you will have a better experience. It may be difficult to relax, more so if you feel stressed or have a busy schedule. When you are starting a visualization session, create an environment that helps you to relax. Focus on your breathing and release the tension from your body. Slow your breath down and lengthen each inhale and exhale. It will help you to relax naturally.

5. Make visualization a regular practice.

Visualization is like most things in life: The more you practice the technique, the more you will reap its benefits. Make visualization a priority by setting aside ten minutes every day to practice. Think of it this way: where you are right now is an accumulation of the choices you have made every day. When you spend time improving your day's quality now, you are not just improving your current life, but your future as well. When it comes to visualization, consistency is vital. This way, you compound the effect of your practice over time.

6. Tap into the emotion of visualization.

Few things are as powerful in creating change as the emotions you experience every time you visualize. When visualizing a moment or a scene, you experience the same emotions and feelings around the moment as if you were living that moment. The ability for visualization to change our lives lies within those emotions and feelings. Whenever you visualize, let whatever emotions and feelings arise come to you and when they do, enjoy them. Allow the emotions to grow within you. After the visualization, take a moment to see how the state of your mind has changed.

The most potent visualizations are those that you experience as most real. To get the most out of your practice, you need a sense of expectation that what you see when you visualize can and will happen for you. You do this by first seeing what you visualize as real in your mind. The more you see and experience those moments from your future, the more the subconscious begins to believe that they will happen. You can visualize anything you would like to achieve in your life, but the following exercise focuses on helping you begin stepping into a future where you are more assertive.

Try this:

Take a moment and close your eyes. Imagine that when you open your eyes, there is a candle in front of you. What is the size of the candle? Is it a taper or a tea candle? How heavy is it? How much of it has burned away? Is it newly lit, or has it burned down to the base? How far away is the candle?

The idea is to get yourself into the present. When you visualize, you are no longer thinking about the future or the past. You are entirely focused on the present. That's all. You are no longer thinking about everyone else—their desires, needs, worries, or expectations of you. For a people-pleaser, visualization is the tiny glimpse that people can live without you worrying about them or being there to help all the time. In practice, your mind has to shut up as you concentrate on the candle. The thoughts you have constantly running in your mind have to stop.

You will likely experience a quiet mind that is so attractive that you will want to keep coming back to it. You will learn self-compassion. One of the attitudes of proper visualization is acceptance—it will help you begin to acknowledge your emotions and pay attention to them. People-pleasers are experts in denying what they feel. They are used to caring for everyone else without having their needs met. They are often out of touch with their emotions. Visualization will help you reconnect with your feelings and truly feel your body's emotions rather than staying stuck in your head. It will help you to process feelings and to let them go.

The surprising thing many people-pleasers do not seem to realize about their behavior is that they are trying to control others in people-pleasing. It seems at odds that the person other people think of as the "giver" is trying to control them. Think about it, though; the people-pleaser is terrified that other people will leave them. They employ their unconscious strategies to control others. Assertiveness training helps you realize that you are not responsible for fixing everything. Part of recovering from people-pleasing is prioritizing your needs and wants. It is learning to set and honor your boundaries. Setting aside time for visualization gives you time and space to dream. You stop focusing on other people's dreams and make yours. You explore different ways of seeing the world.

So far, I encourage you to dare to be better—to be willing to make more self-oriented choices. You want to believe me. You read the first chapter and the second and felt empowered. The certainty inspires you in this book. At some points, you were even moved to tears. The descriptions here seem to match your situation exactly, so why do you still have doubts? Why do you allow fear to cloud your mind and stop your progress? What if self-acceptance, empowerment, and assertiveness are meant for you if you could begin working on it? True, you will have days when it will be difficult not to go back to your default conditioning. You will say yes when you mean no, and you will wonder what to do. If you need a quick fix to get yourself out of the funk or need a self-confidence jolt to motivate you to be better, this section will help you. When you are trying to empower yourself, begin by creating context.

To become the assertive person you want to be, you will need a serious identity upgrade. An upgrade is unlikely to happen if you are still in the places where everyone is used to your people-pleasing. It is naïve to think that you could be stronger than your environment—people generally adjust to their environment; their environment does not adjust to them. When you feel particularly wearied by your people-pleasing tendencies, find a place where you are free to be an independent version of yourself. Enter circumstances that demand you to be this person—it could be anywhere from visiting a shop you have never been to, buying something you want, or moving houses. The idea is to create context first.

Once you are there, allow the organic process of adjusting to unfold. This will be easier for you than trying to defy a context that will be pushing you to be the person you have always been. Remember that it is not enough to feel "bad" that things are not different. While it is essential to feel the impacts of your people-pleasing behavior, you lose your power if you let the feelings of anger, sadness, or fear replace your ability to act. These feelings are simply messengers. They tell you that you want to be different. Acknowledge them, heed the messages, and use them as fuel to make a difference. In the initial steps, remind yourself that no one can do it all. Focus on one or two things that you can do and commit to them fully.

Pick a relationship that you would like to change. Where can you stand up for yourself more? How do you communicate your intent without causing unnecessary damage? Are you willing to do the work? Trust that in changing the small things, you will shift the dynamic of the relationship. The more you see yourself making a difference, the more passionate you will become about improving yourself. Avoid becoming overwhelmed. Ensure you focus only on what you can affect and trust that other people will take care of the things that matter to them.

SUMMARY AND ACTIVITY

If you don't have a seat at the table, you're probably on the menu.

— ELIZABETH WARREN

You will not be given everything you want. In fact, as a people-pleaser, few things you want have been handed to you. You have realized that sometimes you have to go out and get what you want. In this chapter, you have learned what assertiveness is and what it is not. You have seen why you need to speak your mind and how to do it respectfully. You know the value of independence and individuality. Knowing yourself and what you value helps you set boundaries and act when others cross them. You can make sure that you meet your needs first before meeting other people's needs. You are on your way to gaining respect from others.

Activity: Set aside five to ten minutes and find a quiet place to sit. Think of any goal you have in your mind—it can be a relationship that you just realized is toxic and would like to change, an area where you can empower yourself, or even an area of emotional development. What would it feel if you could regulate your emotions better? If you could respond maturely to conflict? What would you think if you succeeded? How would other people respond to you in similar situations? Picture the results you hope for with as much detail as you can.

5

LET'S GAIN SOME RESPECT

We all live in a world filled with conflict. Opinions and worldviews compete against each other. The majority of people believe themselves to be open-minded toward people who see the world differently. We know it is necessary to show respect to those around us, and we genuinely try. Yet, we seem to be lenient toward those who see things our way—this is a human instinct. To push back when we hear someone express a differing opinion is natural, no? Whatever your answer to the question is, we all agree that respect is the glue that holds relationships together. Here, you will learn what it looks like to be respectful and what to do when someone is not respectful toward you.

This chapter will go further than just teaching you how to respect others. One of the reasons your life is not as it should be is that you have missed out on the awkward-sounding but critical skill of setting boundaries. Laying a boundary down involves letting those around you—children, colleagues, lovers, and parents—know of a set of reasonable things that you require to feel happy and respected. It requires informing those around you of these limits in a way that conveys self-possession, confidence, warmth, strength, and kindness.

People who can lay down boundaries successfully will tell their small children that even though they love them dearly, mommy will not want to play another round once a game is over. It will be time to go upstairs to bed—kicking and biting will not make a difference. The adept at setting boundaries will wait until everyone has had their rest to let their partner know that even though they love watching them take the initiative in many areas when it comes to their family, they want to remain in charge. They will explain that their partner does not need to call up his mother-in-law without warning to plan to spend time during the holidays. At work, the manager with boundaries will tell their new hire that though they want to be supportive where they can be, it is not their role to manage budgets or complete schedules for others.

Since most of us do not get an education in this byway of emotional maturity, boundaries are either thrown up destructively or are non-existent. In the case of the people-pleaser, they are too compliant. In the earlier example, the parent fails to admit that they have played enough, and playing late into the night leaves them tired the next day. The child misses the security that comes from knowing that their parent can say no even when it is about something they want badly. In a relationship, they fail to explain what they need to feel content, storing up resentments until they burst into an unexplained rage and exhaust their partner's goodwill. At work, the people-pleaser who lacks boundaries develops the reputation of a friendly pushover.

Invariably, people who cannot lay down boundaries did not have their early boundaries respected. A guardian may not have allowed them to communicate when they were displeased with a difficult situation or someone did not care how hurt their feelings were. Someone might have insinuated that being good and falling in line was the same thing. The people-pleaser has no model for the skill of a winsome and graceful objection.

When it comes to requesting other people to do something for them, the person without boundaries has some anxieties. They fear that they will be hated, receive retribution, or feel like a horrible person if they speak up. Those anxieties manifest as unquestionable certainties. What this view misses is the fact that people rarely hate people who make polite demands. They tend to like them more and respect them. They feel that they are in the presence of a kindly authoritativeness and maturity worthy of their time because it is rare. The people-pleaser forgets that frustrating someone's wishes does not have to point to selfishness. It could signal a noble concern for another's long-term flourishing. You can adore a person, wish them well, have the best intentions toward them, and still decisively tell them no.

Because the people-pleaser does not know what it looks like to have boundaries in place, it is essential to explain what it does not look like. Throwing walls up and getting gratingly defensive is not setting a boundary. The manically defensive person is working with similar fears. They worry that everyone is trying to hurt them; no one would listen unless they respond with immense force, or that their needs can never be truly met. The alternative to lacking boundaries is not violent defensiveness. You should not be dissuaded from boundary-building by its extremes. There is always a way to make a case for your needs without reaching for a weapon.

Notably, the problem of laying boundaries is not very acute with strangers but in intimate relationships. You may be able to fight for your needs with people you care little about but have significant difficulties when dealing with someone you know loves you and who you have allowed into your emotional life. It is as if a part of you cannot reconcile the idea that someone could at once be loving and capable of betraying your best interests. You find it difficult to be intimate and, constantly, a little vigilant. What would help resolve this dilemma is to remember that the same way you can say no and still be kind is the same way another person could remain good, even though they harmed you.

It takes a little courage to notice how bad you may be at setting boundaries. You likely spent a considerable chunk of your life already in passive relationships with daily infringements by those you love. Yet, if little else, I hope that this book so far has taught you that you are not a piece of helpless flotsam on a river, flowing by other's wishes. You have agency and direction. The price for affection is not compliance. You can gradually adopt a seemingly complex but redemptive notion: that you could prove worthy of respect and love, and at the same time, when it is called for, give a warm and definitive "no." To get to this point, you have to understand what respect is and how it looks like in practice.

The dictionary defines respect as a "feeling of deep admiration for something or someone elicited by their achievements, qualities, or abilities." It also includes being aware of other people's wishes and feelings. The word comes from the Latin word respectus which means attention. Respect is an essential component of personal and interpersonal relationships. No wonder feeling respected is in some cases considered a fundamental human right. Respect refers to the ability to honor and value someone else in what they do and say, even if you do not approve of everything they do.

In one sense, respect demands that you accept the other person and stop trying to change them—neither judging them by their behaviors, attitudes, and thoughts nor expecting them to be different. Our differences create our identity. Respect is rooted in the truth that all members of a society are, though different, equal. No wonder oral traditions always included stories that taught children from an early age the value of respect. Everyone becomes due respect because of their humanity. Without respect, interpersonal relationships are filled with dissatisfaction and conflict. Respect allows you to feel safe to express yourself. It eliminates the fear of being discriminated against, judged, or humiliated. It builds safety, well-being, and trust. Yet, respect does not always come naturally. It is something you learn, and it starts with self-respect.

Respecting yourself implies characterizing your incentive and value as a person. If you do not regard yourself, it will be harder to accord others due respect. Everything begins with you. Otherwise referred to as self-esteem, self-respect is crucial to a feeling of well-being. It is odd that for such an essential thing, the allocation of esteem is unpredictable. There are people whose jobs are modest, whose bodies are unspectacular, and whose friends are ordinary but who possess buoyant levels of self-respect. These people seem to like themselves despite the lack of any apparent signs of approval from the world.

No amount of prestige, achievement, or financial security will help the people-pleaser if they do not work on themselves. They chastise themselves anxiously and offer personal critiques, constantly feeling under-performed and never trusting that they deserve to take up space. Having self-respect ultimately has little to do with achieving certain things in life. It is connected with an internal and subjective logic, whose factors seem immune to achievement.

The most significant determinant of your self-respect is how you compare with your parent of the same sex. It seems that comfortable self-respect levels are available only to those who outpace their same-sex parent. If you are from a poor background, you have an unwitting advantage in this case. You might only be driving a beaten-up car, living in one room, but if your same-sex parent struggled more, you at times feel like a prince. Those who grow up in privilege might be unable to shake off the haunting feeling that they are not quite enough.

Self-respect is also often tied to what your peer group is doing. We do not feel inadequate compared to everyone who has more than us, only people who belong to our peer group. This could be people we went to school with, those of the same age, or neighbors. These people matter more to your sense of well-being than the whole population. Finally, self-respect is tied to the kind of love you received as a child. Some people received conditional love—it was all about school reports and grades. They grow up to be high-achievers but have difficulties dealing with their self-hatred. They work to impress everyone they meet in a veiled search to attain the elusive parental approval.

These origins of self-respect interact in different ways with people-pleasing behavior. One thing runs true, though, for all people-pleasers: they have low regard for themselves. Knowing the internal origins of self-esteem frees you from expecting external achievements to fill the hole in your heart. It gives you the key to feeling good about yourself. It changes where you imagine your challenges lie. You stop expecting economic and professional achievements alone to satisfy you. You understand the dynamics of conditionality, shame, and humiliation. Yet, even though high self-esteem is majorly a prize of psychology, there are things you can do to improve yours.

One way to conceptualize yourself in the world is to think of who you are as an inconsequential speck of dust among seven billion others. When you think of yourself this way, it does not matter what you do or what you say. You can conveniently evade taking responsibility because who you are affects nothing in the world. The price you pay for this is to continue in your nihilistic people-pleasing. The alternative way to look at it, which is the fundamental principle behind building your self-respect, is that you exist in a network. There are a thousand people in your network, and this number is continually growing with every social media account, work networking event, or chance bump in at the grocery store. Each of these people knows a thousand other people. It means that you are one person away from a million people and two persons away from many more. You are at the center of that network. If you conceptualize yourself this way, you understand how vital your speech is and how important you are.

The point here is not to draw your self-respect from without but to truly understand the value you bring to the world and use it in evaluating the social factors that often influence self-respect. This work will demand that you constantly work on yourself. You will have to think of your daily habits that seem insignificant because these things make up most of your life. For starters, stop talking down to yourself. Go through your day and watch the way you communicate with yourself. Things like:

"I cannot do this..."
"I am stupid..."

And so forth. These words affect the way you see yourself. Sometimes it may feel like these harsh judgments are necessary, but remaining kind to yourself as you urge yourself forward is necessary for the long run. Replace your negative self-talk with empowering words.

As you begin to stand up for yourself, you will ruffle some feathers, and that is normal—what is not normal, though, is to have people who make you feel bad for valuing your space and time. If you find such people around you, avoid them as much as you can. Being mindful of how you speak to yourself will not mean much if you are surrounded by people who use the same speech with you. Learning self-respect is complicated enough on its own without having toxic people around you. That way, you eliminate the need to second-guess all your words and actions, which works against your efforts to respect yourself.

While at it, stop comparing yourself with other people. In today's ever-connected world, the chances are that you hear stories of people who are doing better than you in one area or another. In mulling over the differences, you start feeling bad because your achievements do not match theirs or begin judging their lifestyles to make yourself feel better. Either way, you are breeding resentment and working against self-respect. Ultimately, self-respect comes from a place where you learn to interact with others, take in their opinions, wishes, and desires and filter them against your values, choosing to empower yourself instead of defining who you are by what they want.

As you build your self-respect, you will become more positive. Suddenly, the world will no longer be a bleak place. You will rid yourself of your negative self-perception and cultivate a positive outlook. You will become more optimistic about your future and the role you play in making it a reality. You will also become more daring. The things you found scary, those that would trigger insecurities, will lose their daunting quality. When you confront your internal discomfort, you will develop the confidence to live outside your bubble. You will build resilience toward criticism. In that sense, self-respect will build your character. You will become more emotionally stable, and other people's thoughts of you will not hold so much weight.

What is more, you will enjoy being with yourself because you will like yourself more. You will no longer feel the need to fill every waking moment with mindless interactions. You will build patience in your relationships and stick with people who are worth your affection and your time. Alongside a sharpened character will be a greater sense of morality. You will become more willing to fight for what you believe to be true. You will slowly lose your concern over people's acceptance and reconcile that the right people will accept you for knowing how to embrace who you are.

You will gain a more remarkable ability to love others and to receive love. You will develop traits that will make you a better friend, sibling, daughter or son, and partner. Other people will take you more seriously, learning from your example. You do, after all, take yourself seriously. Finally, your source of happiness will be internal. You will not need to look outside for validation and happiness. Since this will be your new mode of being, others will sense it and adapt. They will learn to respect you because of the respect you give yourself.

The positive effects of self-respect are many. As discussed in an earlier chapter, you begin by defining your value, upholding your standards, and ensuring that those around you adhere to similar standards. Self-respect is the way you separate yourself from the world without removing yourself from the experience of having a life. It gives you the ability to see your position in the world and your unique value while participating in healthy and meaningful relationships. As you show others that your life has intrinsic meaning, they begin to project the same kind of energy toward you. Before you know it, self-respect has morphed from a self-empowering tool into a personal compass that guides every one of your interactions with the world around you.

As you build your self-respect, you have to learn how to establish and maintain boundaries. If you grew up in an environment where you were taught that being assertive is "cold," "mean" or "rude," the idea of setting boundaries may be unthinkable. The problem is, too much leniency can lead to abuse. When people are not considerate of your emotions, and you let them, you signal to them and yourself that your time, feelings, and efforts are not as important as theirs. Establishing boundaries reinforces your self-respect. The purpose of boundaries is to make it clear "where you end and I begin." They allow each person to express who they are without someone overstepping. Boundaries also provide a sense of structure and predictability, which helps to regulate the nervous system.

Unfortunately, boundaries are not as apparent as a fence with a huge "no trespassing" sign. They are more like invisible bubbles. They are challenging to navigate but essential for our well-being, health, and safety. They give you a sense of agency over your body, physical space, and feelings. We all have limits, and boundaries communicate where the line is. This is to say that you can set your boundaries for your sexuality, personal space, energy and time, thoughts and emotions, possessions, religion, culture, and ethics. Any area you value is fair game.

Yet, setting boundaries and honoring other people's boundaries is not a science. There are ways, though, that you can learn to take charge of your life. While boundaries keep you separate in one sense, they are also the connecting points in relationships. They provide healthy rules for navigating professional and intimate interactions. Boundaries protect relationships from becoming unsafe. They allow you to make yourself a priority. A common misconception people have of boundaries is that they remain the same over time. While some do, others are like water—they ebb and flow. As a rule of thumb, do not draw your boundaries in indelible ink. It is good practice to think about your boundaries often and to reassess them. Otherwise, they will cause problems. Rigid boundaries cause you to become isolated. They could be a reason to give up time with others altogether.

Boundaries allow you to conserve your emotional energy. They protect you from the familiar resentment buildup from people-pleasing and allow you an ability to advocate for yourself. Arguably, you do not need to have the exact boundaries for everyone. If you navigate your boundary-setting well, they will allow you to have a different radius adapted to the person you are interacting with or the situation. You will be able to maintain enough energy to care for yourself. Understand that simply because you love helping your best friend does not mean you also have to carry heavy emotional weight when someone texts you about their latest breakup.

Finally, boundaries allow you space to grow and to be vulnerable. Everyone deals with complex feelings around one area or another. By setting boundaries and breaking them when the time is right, you choose to trust someone with your vulnerability, which creates trust. This could be something as simple as talking to your family and friends openly. When we are vulnerable with someone, we signal to them that they are safe and welcome to open up to us. Yet, vulnerability is not the same as oversharing. Shared vulnerability builds trust and intimacy. Oversharing can use drama to hold people emotionally hostage, manipulate them, or force a relationship in a given direction.

One way to recognize that someone is oversharing is if:

- They post personal attacks and rants on social media
- They share personal details with strangers, trying to hurry the relationship along
- They have no filters for their drama
- They dominate conversations
- They expect on-call emotional support from family and friends

Knowing this difference is critical to setting and communicating your boundaries. An occasional overshare is allowed—everyone has probably done it once in a while. Yet, if you make a habit of it, you are stepping on other people's boundaries. Boundaries clue us into harmful behavior. Think of them as the front door in your apartment. If someone breaks it down, you know there is a significant problem.

Often, people recovering from people-pleasing push their instincts aside because they are convinced they should not feel that way. You fear that you would be unreasonable in trusting your instincts, but it is a red flag if something constantly feels unsafe or uncomfortable. The same way you should not violate other people's boundaries is the same way you should not let them violate yours. Boundaries are deeply personal, meaning that they vary with different people and at different stages of your life. They are shaped by:

- Culture
- Family dynamics
- Life experiences
- Personality

One standard cannot hold for all boundaries. You have to find the level of comfort that works for you with different situations through self-reflection. If you are unsure where to begin, answer the following questions:

1. What are your rights?

Boundaries must factor in your basic human rights. For example, you have a right to say no without feeling guilty, to be treated respectfully, to make your needs as significant as other people's needs, and to be accepting of your failures and mistakes. It is also within your rights to reject meeting other people's unreasonable expectations of you. Once you identify your basic rights and choose to believe them, it will become easier for you to honor them. When you honor your rights, you will spend less time and energy pacifying those who dishonor them.

2. What does your gut say?

Unlike the first question which you can settle once, you have to keep consulting your gut, especially when you are uncertain. Your instincts can prove helpful in determining who is violating your boundaries or where you need to set them up. Consult with your body—stomach, throat, sweating, and tightness in the chest or increased heart rate—to let you know where you need to draw a boundary and what your limits are.

3. What are your values?

In the fourth chapter, you learned how to identify your values. Here, you learn how values relate to your boundaries. Reflect on how often each of the values you identified is tread upon, challenged, or poked in a way that leaves you feeling uncomfortable. This will show you where you need boundaries or where they need to be fortified. If in your reflection you notice that you feel exhausted because of someone or after an activity, note them down as areas to grow in assertiveness. If you set your boundaries with assertiveness, it feels kind but firm to others. Assertive language is non-negotiable and clear.

It does not threaten or blame the recipient. Use "I" statements such as:

- I feel ---- when ---- because ----
- What I need is -----

To safeguard your boundaries, you have to say "no" when it is called for. If you are hesitant about offering more information, it is unnecessary to do that: "No" is a complete sentence. You can say no without explaining or offering any emotional labor to the person receiving it. If someone asks for your number, for example, you can say no. If a coworker asks you to cover their shift, you can say no and do not need to explain.

You can also set boundaries for your possessions and emotional spaces without being required to announce it to the world. Tech devices provide an excellent opportunity for this. For example, a password-protected journal is a boundary, and so is putting your phone on airplane mode when you need alone time to recharge. The idea is to do whatever is necessary to make it easy to meet your needs. You can schedule non-negotiable alone time and use it to do your own thing, or you can temporarily suspend messaging apps when you do not want to be contacted. Research shows that everyone, not just recovering people-pleasers, should take time to be alone. Just the expectation that you should be available to answer a work email during non-work hours can decrease well-being and cause friction in relationships (Becker et al., 2018).

Today's tech-savvy world has introduced dimensions to boundary-setting that might not have been an issue a few decades ago. Tech spaces increasingly cause issues in romantic relationships. How often have you heard complaints from one partner about their loved one's love for social media? Technology has paved the way for control and an invasion of privacy. People go so far as to use communication technology to monitor or manipulate their spouse or significant other. As an adult, it is your right to secure your data and to keep your messages private. Among other boundaries, you need to develop a habit of communicating digital device boundaries.

Asserting your boundaries can get trickier if your loved one lives with anxiety, depression, mental illness, or has a history of trauma. You could see their struggles in managing their emotions, and that triggers your people-pleasing tendencies, causing you to allow them to overstep your boundaries in the name of providing relief. How do you handle boundary setting in a situation like that? It is not easy to provide the specific boundaries you need because you cannot anticipate all the instances that may need boundaries. For instance, a sexual assault survivor may have a boundary that they prefer to be asked before being touched. After they get comfortable with a person, they could break that boundary for the sake of intimacy. Suppose you are still experiencing challenges with setting or asserting boundaries. In that case, it may be because you either have not fully understood what healthy boundaries look like or that you do not know you need boundaries in specific areas.

Sometimes, people are not trying to cross your boundaries, they are simply not aware of those limits. Often, for the recovering people-pleaser, it is because you are not clear with yourself about what you need. The following are six boundaries that you deserve and some examples of what they could look like:

1. Physical boundaries

Everyone needs personal space, and that need is influenced by your comfort with touch and other physical needs like thirst, hunger, and the need for rest. Violations to physical boundaries feel like receiving unwanted touches or being denied your physical needs. They exist on a spectrum, with the most severe violations causing neglect or serious physical abuse. It is okay to tell people around you that you need more space. It is okay to tell them when you need rest or are hungry. A healthy physical boundary might sound like:

- "I am not a hugger. Handshake?"
- "I am allergic to meat, so I cannot have that in my house."
- "I feel really tired. I need a seat."
- "No, do not touch me that way."
- "Please always ask before going into my room."

2. Emotional boundaries

Emotional boundaries help you to honor and respect your energy and feelings. Setting emotional boundaries means recognizing your emotional limits, knowing when to reveal and when to hide, and limiting emotional sharing with poor responders. It means validating other people's feelings. Criticizing other people's feelings can be an emotional boundary violation, and so could reading someone's journal, asking inappropriate questions, assuming you know other people's feelings, and emotional dumping. An emotional boundary might sound like this:

- "I am having a hard time and I need to talk. Are you in the right mental space to listen?"
- "When I let you in on my feelings and you are critical, I shut down. I can only share if you are respectful in your responses."
- "I am sorry you are going through a rough patch, but right now, I am not able to hear you out. Could we please take this up later?"
- "Now is not the right time for that conversation."

3. Time boundaries

Time may not be money, but it is a crucial resource that needs protection. Setting time boundaries will allow you to be more effective at work, socially, and in your family life. It means understanding what is a priority and allocating time to it without overcommitting. You understand which relationships need your time and which can get by with a phone call. A time boundary violation could be anything from giving your time as a professional without being paid and canceling on people because you overcommitted to keeping conversations going long past an appropriate end and contacting unavailable people. A healthy time boundary looks like this:

- "I am only available for thirty minutes."
- "Do you have time for a chat today?"
- "Saturdays are family time, so I will not be available."
- "I would love to help, but can I do so another time?"
- "I am happy to come. My hourly rate is…"

4. Sexual boundaries

Sexual boundaries clarify issues like consent and agreement, and they communicate preferences, privacy, respect, and desires. They include discussing what you find exciting, saying no to hurtful things, protecting your privacy, and discussing contraception. In a sexually charged society, sexual boundary violations often become easy to miss. Still, they include everything from sulking and punishing someone who does not want to have sex to unwanted touch, rape, or assault. Leering is crossing a sexual boundary, and so is lying about your sexual history. Unwanted sexual comments are certain violations of sexual boundaries. A healthy sexual boundary might be:

- "Are you comfortable with this?"
- "I don't like that. Let's try something else."
- "What do you like?"

- "I am too tired tonight. Can we just cuddle?"
- "I am into … Are you comfortable with it?"

5. Intellectual boundaries

Intellectual boundaries protect your curiosity, ideas, and thoughts as well as those of other people. They are violated when your thoughts are dismissed, shut down, or belittled. Here, it is vital to differentiate between healthy and unhealthy conversations. If someone is sexist or racist in their speech, you have a right to draw a rigid boundary. You do not need to have an "intellectual" conversation with them. A good rule of thumb is to ask: Does this conversation violate other people? Healthy intellectual boundaries might sound like:

- "Whenever we have this conversation, we end up angry. I think it is good to avoid this right now."
- "I can respect our differences on this."
- "I know we do not see eye to eye, but you do not have to belittle me."

The more you set boundaries, the more you will learn to recognize them. In boundary setting, you help others show up for you and sharpen your ability to be there for them—in the famous words of Brené Brown: Clear is kind.

So far, my goal has been to help you set boundaries to make it easier for people to meet your needs. Yet, in your recovery, you will cross other people's boundaries as well. How do you recognize when people around you have set boundaries, and how do you honor them? There are three beginner rules you can use to guide you to be mindful of others, including:

1. Look out for cues.

Social cues provide a glimpse into other people's boundaries. When engaged in a conversation with someone and they move back when you step forward, you receive information about how comfortable they are with closeness. Hints that someone might need more space include avoiding eye contact, backing up, turning away, and giving one-word responses. Watch for other signs like flinching, a stiffening posture, excessive nodding, and nervous gestures like laughing.

2. Be aware of neurodiverse responses.

Cues are not the same for everyone. Bear in mind that some people use certain gestures regularly, which disqualifies the gestures as clues into their psyche. In such cases, you may have to look for other cues. The term "neurodiverse" refers to those who are on the autism spectrum or people with developmental disabilities. Their social cues often differ from the norm.

3. Ask.

Allowing yourself to ask for clarification when in doubt can clear things up for you quickly. You can inquire if it is okay with someone to hug them or ask a personal question. As you ask, be prepared to accept whatever response you get.

Wherever you are in your people-pleasing recovery, permit yourself to muddle things up once in a while. Self-doubt, fear, and guilt are huge potential pitfalls. You might fear other people's responses if you enforce your boundaries. You might feel guilty for speaking up or turning down a family member's request. Your default will be to assume that you should say yes because you are a nice person. You will likely wonder whether you deserve boundaries in the first place. Remind yourself that boundaries are not just a sign of health: they are a sign of self-respect. Permit yourself to set them and to preserve the boundaries you have set.

When the situation arises, as it certainly will, where you cannot identify your feelings in order to honor them, ask yourself what has changed. Consider what you are doing and what is happening around you. Mull over your options and figure out what you have control over. You might even benefit from visiting your past to compare it with your present. Are you slipping into your caretaker role with a parent instead of preserving a boundary? Have you allowed yourself to ignore your needs? Have you allowed relationships back into your life that are not reciprocal?

Beyond relationships, it could be that you have stepped into an unhealthy environment. Are you yielding to the implicit expectation that you extend your work hours? Do you surround yourself with people without healthy boundaries? Tune into your feelings and prioritize self-care if that is the case. Self-care means that you recognize how important your feelings are as cues to your wellbeing. By putting yourself first, you give yourself the peace of mind and energy to be more present with others. You empower yourself to be a better friend, coworker, husband, or mother.

If things prove difficult, seek support. You can pursue counseling, good friendships, or the support of a coach. The idea is to let someone else in on the fact that you are having difficulties setting boundaries. Having someone in your corner will allow you to be more assertive. They will act as your secure base, freeing you to explore out of your comfort zone. They will encourage you to communicate when a situation is particularly bothersome and work with you to address it. They will help you to start small.

Like every other new skill, setting and maintaining your boundaries takes practice. Begin small, with a non-threatening target, and work incrementally to boundaries you find more challenging. Build upon your successes rather than jumping into something you find overwhelming. Build the courage to be better, and remember that boundary-keeping is a skill you can master.

SUMMARY AND ACTIVITY

When you start loving yourself and respecting your time and energy... your value will go up.

— GERMANY KENT

In this chapter, you have learned how to respect yourself and, as a result, respect others. You know how to set boundaries with yourself and others and how to honor and preserve them. You have learned how to avoid busting other people's boundaries and healthy communication around boundaries. You realize that setting boundaries is a skill that you pick up and build with patience and courage. You have all you need to set and assert your value. Others will follow your example.

Activity: In your self-reflection space, ask yourself what your life would look like if you set boundaries. What relationships would change, and how? You can go further and journal your reflections. What are you currently doing to promote self-respect? What have you learned that you can start implementing, and how will you go about it?

6

EVERYDAY CONFIDENCE

Whatever the goal, the difference between failure and success often hangs on a concept few people talk about: confidence. This final chapter walks you around the issues that stop you from making more of yourself. It discusses imposter syndrome and goal setting. It borrows lessons from some historical figures on courage and resilience to help you regard confidence no more as a matter of luck, but as something you can improve, that indeed, you must. Confidence is a skill. You can learn its secrets. It can be jarring to find out just how many great things have been done in the world, not as a result of excellent talent or technical skill, but through courage.

Many of the world's education systems are set up in a way that students spend a lot of time becoming confident in technical fields like economics or mathematics. Still, the need to acquire a wider variety of confidence is often ignored. Yet, if met, such confidence can serve us across different tasks, from arranging a marriage proposal to speaking to strangers at networking events. It could empower us to change the world. People often lack confidence because they think of it as something you either have or do not have. Some people are very confident for mysterious reasons. In contrast, others, like us, are stuck with the confidence levels our genetics accord us.

The opposite is also true. Confidence is not a divine gift. It is a skill based on ideas about the world and where we fall into it. These ideas can be studied and learned so that they uproot compliance and hesitancy. You can school yourself in confidence. Here, the point is not just to draw your attention to the things you do well, even if that could be one aspect of confidence. Thinking only of your experience, competence, and intelligence as the reason to be confident can have awkward consequences. There is an "under-confidence" that follows too much attachment to one's dignity. You become anxious around some people or a situation that seems to threaten your dignity, and you hold back from challenges that have a risk. Of course, this compromises the very thing you are trying to encourage —confidence.

In a work networking meeting, you become reluctant to request help finding the washrooms because other people might think you are a naïve, pitiable newcomer. You fail to apply for promotions at work in case the management finds you arrogant. In love, you long for a kiss but never abandon the fear that you could be seen as an opportunistic loser. To never appear foolish, you never leave your comfort zone, missing out on the best things life has to offer. At the heart of the under-confidence I refer to, you have a skewed picture of the dignity of an ordinary person. You imagine that past a particular age, you are beyond mockery. You start to think that you can live well without sometimes making a fool of yourself.

Erasmus once said that everyone, however learned they are, is a fool. There are no exceptions. Your passions may once in a while get the better of you. You fall prey to irrational fear; you are clumsy at elegant parties or make a wrong judgment. In one sense, folly is part of human existence. One mistake people-pleasers make when trying to recover from people-pleasing is to over-emphasize their good qualities, which are often many, so much so that they develop this type of under-confidence that assumes an irrational amount of dignity. They forget that some repeated idiocies do not make them any less dignified. Making the occasional mistake does not make you unfit for society.

The way to greater confidence is not just to reassure yourself of your dignity but also to become confident in the inevitable nature of your idiocies. There are no other options available to people. You will become timid if you let yourself be very familiar with other people's respectable sides. In the social media world, for example, most people constantly put their best foot forward. They take great pains to seem normal and success-ful, creating a ghost that suggests a "normal" that is simply not possible. Once you learn to see yourself as, by nature, a little clumsy, it ceases to matter if you do one more thing that makes you look naïve. The person directing you to the washroom might treat you with contempt, but that would not be news. You already gracefully accepted that you are human. In such a full embrace of the self, you remove the sting of trying and failing. You reduce the fear of humiliation and set yourself free to try things and see failure as normal. Often, amidst the failures, you get satisfying successes you would never have imagined.

Becoming more confident starts with reminding yourself as often as you need to that you are just as human as everyone else. One act of folly, no matter how major it seems to you, should not matter much. Yet, as simple as this truth sounds, something else often presents as a challenge for you to overcome—the impostor syndrome. Recovering people-pleasers often leave the possibility of succeeding to others, unable to see themselves as the kind of people who make it. When they attempt to set boundaries with the idea of becoming more responsible, they easily convince themselves that they are "impostors"—like actors in a poorly written play.

The impostor syndrome stems from an unhelpful picture of what successful people are like. You feel like an impostor, not because you are familiar with your flaws but because you cannot imagine anyone else to be less than their polished surface. Some traces of impostor syndrome go as far back as childhood. To a five-year-old, it seems impossible that their father was ever their age, inexperienced with the kitchen knife, and unable to decide other people's leisure activities and bedtimes. The status gap seems unbridgeable. The child loves video games and bouncing on the sofa, and those are nothing like talking on the phone for hours while sipping on a beer. They start their life with the impression that the people they admire are not like them at all.

This experience in childhood, uncorrected, becomes a view of the human condition. You know your inside and others only from outside. You are ever aware of your doubts and anxieties but know others by what they tell you, which is an edited version. You conclude that you must be a worse human being. But really, you are simply failing to see that others are as fragile as you are. You do not have to know the exact thing that cracks someone's polished exterior to know that there is something. You might not be familiar with their regrets, but you can trust they have deep feelings. You can believe this because compulsions and vulnerabilities are a universal feature of the human mind. How then do you deal with the impostor syndrome? Take a leap of faith. Believe that other people's minds work just like yours. Everyone has some uncertainties and anxieties, just like you do.

Taking a leap of faith around others helps you to humanize them. When faced with a seemingly formidable person, you are not really encountering them that way, but you see someone who, despite evidence to the contrary, is very much like yourself in some ways. Confidence means seeing through the myth of who people seem to be in order to recognize their humanity. With this recognition begins the efforts to bridge the gap between history and the present. One of the things standing between confident people and those who are less so is their approach to history—the unconfident think of history as having passed. The confident know that history is still being made, and they have a chance to be part of it every day.

The world around us suggests that everything is already settled—you imagine that the status quo is set. On one side, you see people more accomplished than you, who follow traditions that have existed for centuries. You constantly hear reasons why things are as they are and are encouraged to embrace them. It is not surprising that you come to believe that everything possible has already been fully mapped. The result is that you can hardly imagine alternatives. What is the point of beginning a new venture when the market is already full? Why should you be loyal to a new idea?

History, though, proves that things change often, and they change sharply. New continents are discovered, nations pioneer other ways of government, dress and style change, and so does worship. Theoretically, you come away from this knowledge being aware that change is constant. In practice, unless you are intentional, you distance yourself from your society and a daily belief that you are in an ever-changing story and are currently a central actor. You forget that history is what is happening around you. The point here is that your present has all the contingency of the past. It is just as malleable. Current habits seem firm, but that is only because you exaggerate how fixed they are. You can wake up every day and trust in your power to join the flow of history and change its direction.

One of the familiar sources of despair for people in their personal development is the belief that things should be easier than they are. You give up, not because of the difficulty, but because you did not expect it. You interpret the struggle as shameful proof that you do not have what you need to become more assertive. You grow subdued, and eventually you surrender because the struggle seems rare. The capacity to stay the course will be demanded of you. It is, in a sense, internalizing the right story about the difficulties you can expect, which is why this section of the book is necessary. Often, the stories we begin our journey to become better with work against us—they are deeply misleading. Most are tied to the media narrative that success is an overnight occurrence.

Sometimes, the successful person imagines that if they tell the real story of the grit and sweat it took to get where they are, they might discourage others, and so they give you an edited snapshot of their highs. Other times, the reasons behind the unrealistic stories are more self-serving—impressing people. The successful artist may hide their labors to make their job seem inevitable and natural, for example. The issue with this approach is that when it comes to doing the actual things, and in this case, growing away from people-pleasing, you see your failures as proof of your inability. Without an accurate map for development, you are unable to position yourself properly next to your defeat.

No wonder I deliberately talk about the challenges you may expect in your efforts to practice what you have learned in this book. The idea is to prepare you for the hardships you will meet so that when you are there, working to better who you are, you will be ready. Preparedness is a part of confidence. That way, you can set realistic expectations. Your setbacks will take on a different meaning. Confidence is not the belief that you will not have to cross obstacles. It is recognizing that obstacles are part of anything worth doing.

One of the obstacles you may need to overcome earlier is finding out that someone intensely dislikes you even though you did not provoke them. The people-pleaser finds this lesson incredibly difficult. Enemies do not need to be a catastrophe. You will need to face the fact that the world's approval should not support your approval of yourself. The confident person knows that every decent person will have a few enemies as they live their life.

You will also need to overcome self-sabotage. The people-pleaser does not naturally seek out their happiness. Because this has been ingrained in you for so long, you may find that you deliberately sabotage your chances of having your needs met. When this happens, remind yourself that you can, despite your fears, survive disappointment. Take a few moments and reflect on what is happening. You might find that you find the idea of confidence unappealing. You find the truly confident to be offensive without fully realizing it because you assume it to be the opposite of modesty. People-pleasers might, for example, take pride in the fact that they do not complain about bad services, they do not fuss about salaries, or ask friends to rearrange their schedules. Their meekness protects some associations they have made over time with self-assertion. It will feel as if, to be a moral citizen, you have to avoid explicit assertions of your interest. You must fight this way of thinking. It is not enough to be exciting and intelligent on the inside; you have to develop the confidence to help you be active in the world. It is the skill that puts the theories into practice.

Now that you understand the psychology of confidence, there are practical things you can do in your daily life to build your confidence. Overall, confidence is built on accomplishments and choices that feed the things you love and give you a sense of pride.

1. Do the things that are important to you.

Confidence is not built only on accomplishment, but accomplishment is a huge part of it. As a people-pleaser, you have done things for the sake of others. Part of becoming an individual is doing the things that are important to you. As you achieve the small goals you set for yourself, you feel better. Set a goal every day—something that if you did today, your day would not just be better, but so would your future. Make the tasks small enough that they are not overwhelming, but big enough that they make a difference. Bear in mind that your progress has to be incremental. Significant changes do not take place overnight. You will feel like retooling your personality is ambiguous if you think of it in general, but as you set small relational goals, it will appear achievable and increase your belief that it is doable.

You will need to be keen as you set your goals. Ensure that they are things that genuinely make you happy—factor in even the things you do with your spare time. Whatever it is that you love, make time for it, and you will be your best self that way. As you work toward those goals, monitor your progress. If your goal today was to tell your sister that you cannot help her with her baby next week and you manage to do it, tick it off your list as work well done. When trying to get a promotion, change careers, or lose weight, monitor your progress. Do your best to quantify the achievements you make. You can even reward yourself. It will help you build confidence to see real-time progress as a result of your efforts. If you are uncertain of what to do, consult your values as identified in chapter four, then choose based on your value system. This will help you to always do the right thing by yourself. It will refine your character and encourage you to become a better version of yourself.

2. Take care of your body.

It is not easy to love yourself if you are in the habit of abusing your body. If you care for yourself, you know that you care for your spirit, body, and mind and naturally feel confident. Watch what you eat. A good diet is good for your self-esteem. Eating the right foods makes you feel stronger, healthier, and more energized. You also need to make time for exercise. Regular exercise improves your body image, which increases your confidence. Exercise also helps with memory retention, stress management, and improved focus. It is more difficult to fall into anxiety with excess energy to draw upon.

3. Practice self-compassion.

Self-compassion is about showing kindness to yourself whenever you fail, make a mistake, or meet an obstacle. Failing is not your enemy. Self-compassion is how to relate with yourself to be emotionally flexible, face the challenging emotions you experience, and connect with yourself and others. Self-compassion contributes to confidence. It comes from the recognition that failure is part of life.

4. Be prepared.

I cannot overestimate the importance of being prepared. The most successful people do not just happen upon success. They have put in the work to be where they are. Preparation will mean different things depending on the circumstance you are in. It may mean running a text by a friend before sending it to someone when setting a boundary, or it could mean practicing a speech you need to make before board members. Preparation is also tied to following through. People respect those who follow through with what they said they would do. More importantly, you respect yourself and believe in yourself a little more because action gives meaning to words.

Preparation will help you to face things you would otherwise put off. People often put off pursuing some goals until they feel more confident, but you often gain that confidence by doing. Preparation will help you face your fears. It will balance your self-doubt, but be careful not to expect 100% confidence before you allow yourself to do things. You might never get there.

5. Practice mindfulness.

Mindfulness is about being present. It is an awareness of where you are and your actions there. When you are mindful, you are not overwhelmed or overly reactive to what is happening around you. Whenever you bring to conscious awareness what you are experiencing through your senses or acknowledge your emotions and thoughts, you are being mindful. Research shows that when you train your mind to be mindful, you remodel its physical structure. The goal is to wake up your inner workings and be alive to your emotional, mental, and physical processes.

Some popular ideas around mindfulness, though, miss the point. When you start to practice it, you will likely find the experience different from your expectation. You will be pleasantly surprised. Mindfulness is not about fixing you or stopping your thoughts. It is neither a religious reserve nor an escape from reality, and it is certainly not a panacea. Mindfulness is more than stress management. Stress reduction often results from the practice of mindfulness, but it is not the goal. Mindfulness teaches your body to thrive. All over the world, athletes use mindfulness to make sure they perform their best. It coaches the whole person.

Mindfulness will also boost your creativity. Whether it is coloring, drawing, or even writing in your journal as an accompanying meditative practice, mindfulness will help your creative process. It strengthens neural connections. In training your brain to be mindful, you build new networks and neural pathways, boosting awareness and flexibility, all of which make you more confident.

SUMMARY AND ACTIVITY

From this chapter, you have learned that no one is born with the confidence they need to be active in the world. However, some factors impact us and form a pattern that becomes part of the way we interact with reality. Your current confidence levels are a function of your environment and your upbringing, but are not permanent. You can build up your confidence by:

- Doing the things that matter to you
- Taking care of your body

- Preparedness
- Surrounding yourself with the right people
- Practicing self-compassion and accepting the reality of failure
- Practicing mindfulness

Activity: The activities provided at the end of every chapter in this book are meant to help you reflect on yourself using the newly acquired knowledge. This final chapter takes a different approach. It aims to teach you a basic meditation practice that you can use to practice mindfulness every day. This practice focuses on your breath, not because it is special, but because the physical breathing sensation is always there. You always have access to it so that you can use it any time to anchor yourself to your present. Through the practice, you may find yourself dwelling on the sounds around you, your emotions, or your thoughts. Wherever your mind goes, allow it to do so before coming back again to the next breath.

Find a place you feel comfortable at and pick a solid and stable seat. Notice what is happening with your legs—if you picked a cushion, cross your legs in front of you. If you picked a chair, rest your feet on the floor. Straighten your upper body without stiffening. Your spine has a natural curve—allow it to stay that way. Notice what you are doing with your arms. Put them parallel to your upper body and rest your palms on your legs as it feels natural to you. Drop your chin and soften your gaze. You may close your eyes if you like—only let what appears before your eyes remain there without focusing on it.

Focus your attention on your breath. Feel the physical sensation of breathing. How is the air moving through your mouth or nose? Observe the rising of your chest or belly. Notice when your mind wanders to things other than your breath. Inevitably, this will happen. Do not worry. Do not try to eliminate thinking. When your mind wanders, gently return your focus to your breath. Be kind with yourself if your mind keeps wandering. It is typical for beginners. Rather than fighting your thoughts, observe them without reacting. Simply sit and focus. It will not be easy, but that is all there is. Keep returning to your breath without expectation or judgment. When you are ready, lift your gaze gently. If you had closed your eyes, you could open them. Notice any movement or sounds in your environment. How does your body feel? What thoughts and emotions do you have?

Whenever you start to feel overwhelmed or out of touch with your feelings, perform this meditation practice to center yourself and make the next choice that comes to you based on your gut feeling.

7

SHORT ANSWERS TO FREQUENTLY ASKED QUESTIONS

1. How does people-pleasing differ from being a decent person?

People-pleasing is not the same as being a thoughtful and empathetic person concerned about other people's emotional well-being and needs. People-pleasers can appear that way, but their people-pleasing habit causes resentment. They may seem kind and compassionate, but their good deeds often come from a desire to control others and a dependence on external validation. People-pleasers prioritize other people's needs at their own expense. They say "yes" when they mean to say "no."

A people-pleaser will smile and say, "I am happy to come and pick you up on Monday," but on that day, they wake up wondering why they said yes. They will resent that their whole day is cut short because they have to be in traffic waiting for you. The people-pleaser assumes that some debt is created once they do something good for you, and you are expected to reciprocate later.

2. Where does people-pleasing come from?

The short answer is that the people-pleaser once had to please an inconsistent caregiver. As adults, they seem extra-caring and generous. One might think that people-pleasers are easy because they have a big heart, but that is not really where they are coming from. People-pleasers contort themselves to meet others' expectations because they want acceptance, praise, and love. Displeasure feels horrible. Explained that way, people-pleasing can be a form of manipulation.

3. Why does people-pleasing affect more women than men?

Men seem to have an easier time being blunt, communicating assertively, and saying no without apologies. It could be connected to biology or socialization. When threatened, you either flee or fight. This is a universal response for both men and women. Women, however, have another stress response. They tend to befriend, which researchers say is more adaptive for someone who had to care for vulnerable children. It is the quality of being nurturing in women that makes them more prone to people-please.

4. How important is it to say no, and how do I go about it?

Learning to give a gracious no is one of the vital skills every adult needs. It is kinder to be honest than to agree to something that breeds resentment. It has more integrity to turn it down. People-pleasers have a hard time reconciling with the fact that their behavior gives the wrong impression to others. They are lying all the time. To become better at saying no, recall when you last agreed to something you did not want to do. Imagine you had said no—what would be so bad about it and what do you fear? You will most likely find that you are afraid of their disapproval or that they will think you selfish. Acknowledge that fear and then weigh it against the resentment, irritation and dislike you felt agreeing to something you did not want to do. Accept that you do not owe anyone anything and say no when you need to. You will find that you can say yes with more freedom and accommodate others with joy.

5. How do I let go of other people's opinions of me?

There is no easy way to free yourself of other people's opinions. You will have to put in the work to become more assertive and confident. There is an easy answer, though. Remind yourself that you cannot control what other people think or feel about you. You think you can, but it is their thoughts about what you do that cause their emotions. They, like you, can decide to think thoughts that hurt, or they can stay neutral. The only thing you can control is the way you present yourself in the world. Live by your values instead. Let love, integrity, self-acceptance, excellence, and courage guide your behavior.

6. I am trying to overcome people-pleasing. What advice would you give me?

Breaking the people-pleasing habit can be challenging—always remember that you have a choice. Remove "should" from your vocabulary and replace it with "could." Rather than saying "I should volunteer to help the needy," say "I could volunteer to help the needy." That way, you can ask the real question: Is volunteering motivated by my values or by my fears? If you are not sure what the answer to that question is, err on the side of caution. It is always a good idea to stall before saying yes. Use that time to ask yourself whether the choice you are about to make lines up with your values. If this sounds difficult, acknowledge that people-pleasing is a form of dishonesty, and you will see things a little bit clearer.

7. I am not sure whether I am a people-pleaser. How can I know?

Take the test earlier in this book and assess yourself against the answers.

8. Why is people-pleasing terrible for my health and relationships?

People-pleasing is detrimental because you are not true to yourself. Other people may not even know you. They are focused on their wants and needs, and so you become invisible in their lives, and your relationships become one-sided. People-pleasers also internalize their emotions without validating their experiences. According to research, if you do not express yourself or do not recognize your experiences, it can cause inflammation in the body that creates other health issues. You become more susceptible to anxiety and stress because you carry other people's responsibilities. You burn out eventually.

In relationships, people-pleasing is detrimental because you do not show up for the other person. You do not speak up when hurt or when someone crosses your boundary. Over time, you no longer know your boundaries, so you begin feeling resentful, stuck, and underappreciated. You end up ending relationships, or you blow up. All the while, you feel disconnected from yourself and others.

9. Is people-pleasing the same as codependency?

Codependency is an excessive psychological or emotional reliance on a partner. Initially it referred to people with addiction or an illness, but over time, the definition has broadened. The person who is codependent is not the one with the illness, but the one whom they rely upon. The sick person has a valid reason to rely on someone else, but the person for whom they rely upon is just reliant on the illness to meet their desire to be needed. A codependent person needs to feel needed even if it makes them upset to imagine someone potentially taking advantage of them. Codependents are people-pleasers but not all people-pleasers are codependents.

People-pleasing hinges on managing other people's feelings to feel safe. In this book, you have learned what it looks like in practice. The people-pleaser begins as a parent-pleaser. Sociotropic behaviors evolve as a way to keep close with caregivers who are rarely available to their children. Often, these parents are too concerned with their own troubles to see what their child is thinking or feeling, or they mislabel the child's feelings. Since the people-pleaser's parents are often too overwhelmed to be the caregiver in their relationship with their child, the child learns to act as the adult, which eventually strains the relationship between caregiver and child.

Over time, the people-pleasing child learns that their caregiver is unreliable, but she cannot stop depending on them. She learns to prop them up emotionally and to track their moods. The goal? To make their caregiver proud while muffling her needs and doing the best she can not cause trouble. Initially, it is parental inconsistency that results in people-pleasing. The child starts to live her parent's dreams and adopts their values in order to receive care. She loses interest in exploring who she is and starts learning what others expect her to be.

A people-pleasing child carries their habits into their adult relationships. They always try to please others, hanging their happiness there. Adult people-pleasers know how to check the temperature of a room to blend in so that they fit in. They intuit other people's thoughts, needs, and feelings and, by default, care for others to their detriment. You have learned how people-pleasing is often accompanied by low self-esteem, a need for control, and perfectionistic tendencies.

The people-pleaser is constantly preoccupied with others' thoughts and feelings, hungry for their approval, fearful of saying no, neglectful of their needs, and stuck in relationships where they over-give. They end up overworked, exhausted, and burned out, in addition to the resentment they feel against those close to them. Yet, people-pleasing does not have to be a life sentence. You have learned ways to be assertive, gain respect, and live every day with confidence. You know how to figure out what you want and what happiness looks like for you.

You are aware that you can rise above your upbringing with a bit of courage and slowly work out of your ingrained people-pleasing habits. You can connect with your values, identify your dreams and begin to set boundaries with others so you can reach your goals. You can slowly begin finding the confidence to speak your truth, and with practice, what you thought was impossible for you can become your reality. As a recovering people-pleaser, you need to reclaim your inner voice and identify your needs. You know how to label your feelings and use them as guideposts to prioritize your needs.

Now, you can permit yourself to get inspired and excited by what you truly believe. Sometimes, when your desires are buried under fear—more so the fear of not meeting other people's expectations—you can dig beneath that fear and mentally remove yourself from the systems that propagate it. You can identify what needs changing through journaling, self-reflection, and meditation. You have everything you need to weave a web of impact. You can now participate in the making of history by speaking your truth assertively. You know how to get your needs met and how to meet other people's needs from a place of self-love. You have everything you need to overcome people-pleasing, become assertive, and gain respect. Go ahead and do it. Achieve the impossible. And while at it, you can help uplift someone else by leaving a review of this book on Amazon so that others, too, can learn what you have.

REFERENCES

Be wary of "people pleasing" it can ruin your health. (2017, April 1). Lea Stening Health. https://www.leastening.com/articles/motivation/be-wary-of-people-pleasing-it-can-ruin-your-health.html

Becker, W. J., Belkin, L., & Tuskey, S. (2018). *Killing me softly: Electronic communications monitoring and employee and spouse well-being. Academy of Management Proceedings, 2018*(1), 12574. https://doi.org/10.5465/ambpp.2018.121

Bruch, M. A., Rivet, K. M., Heimberg, R. G., Hunt, A., & McIntosh, B. (1999). *Shyness and Sociotropy: Additive and Interactive Relations in Predicting Interpersonal Concerns. Journal of Personality, 67(2), 373–406.* doi:10.1111/1467-6494.00059

Duval, S., & Wicklund, R. A. (1972). *A theory of objective self-awareness.* Academic Press.

Friedman, M. A., & Whisman, M. A. (1998). *Sociotropy, autonomy, and bulimic symptomatology*. International Journal of Eating Disorders, 23(4), 439–442. https://doi.org/10.1002/(sici)1098-108x(199805)23:4<439::aid-eat12>3.0.co;2-r

Milgram, S. (2017). *Obedience to authority*. HarperCollins.

Palmer, B. (2005). *Concepts of eating disorders. Handbook of Eating Disorders*, 1–10. https://doi.org/10.1002/0470013443.ch1

Pedlow, C. T., & Niemeier, H. M. (2013). *Sociotropic cognition and eating disordered attitudes and behavior in young adults. Eating Behaviors, 14(2),* 95–101. doi:10.1016/j.eatbeh.2012.10.001

Ridley, D. S., Schutz, P. A., Glanz, R. S., & Weinstein, C. E. (1992). *Self-regulated learning: The interactive influence of metacognitive awareness and goal-setting. The Journal of Experimental Education*, 60, 293–306.

Rubin, K. H., & Coplan, R. J. (2010). *The development of shyness and social withdrawal*. Guilford Press.

Sato, T., McCann, D., & Ferguson-Isaac, C. (2004). *Sociotropy—Autonomy and Situation-Specific Anxiety. Psychological Reports, 94(1),* 67–76. doi:10.2466/pr0.94.1.67-76

Silvia, P. J., & O'Brien, M. E. (2004). *Self-awareness and constructive functioning: Revisiting "the human dilemma."*

Journal of Social and Clinical Psychology, 23(4), 475–489. https://doi.org/10.1521/jscp.23.4.475.40307

Steiner, S. (2019, November 25). *Top five regrets of the dying.* The Guardian. https://www.theguardian.com/lifeandstyle/2012/feb/01/top-five-regrets-of-the-dying

Sutton, A. (2016). *Measuring the effects of self-awareness: Construction of the Self-Awareness Outcomes Questionnaire.* Europe's *Journal of Psychology, 12,* 645–658.

www.ingramcontent.com/pod-product-compliance
Lightning Source LLC
Chambersburg PA
CBHW021323060726
47591CB00006B/1850